Keep at It, Riley! is a wonderful piece of practical theology. Noreen McInnes infuses her real-life experience into the narrative of sacramental theology and succeeds in integrating her academic studies with her personal faith. There are some passages that moved me to tears, while at other times her wonderful sense of humor had me howling with laughter. I commend her for this important work.

Michael S. Driscoll, Professor Emeritus of Theology, University of Notre Dame

Keep at It, Riley! is an Irish sweater woven with sacraments, Irish spirituality, and family stories. McInnes's life experiences shed light on the value of Catholic ritual in real time. A great read!

Most Reverend John P. Dolan, Auxiliary Bishop of San Diego

In a world that often pushes death and suffering to the margins, Noreen McInnes proposes another possibility: welcoming the sick, the suffering, and, yes, the dying, into the center of our lives. Part family history, part memoir, *Keep at It, Riley!* weaves together personal experience and theological reflection to illuminate God's nearness to us. Anyone who has accompanied a loved one to the threshold of this life will recognize McInnes' honesty, humor, and humility as marks of deep faith.

Jessica Keating Floyd, Program Director, Office of Life and Human Dignity, University of Notre Dame

In *Keep at It, Riley!*, Noreen Madden McInnes has skillfully woven into a deeply personal testimony to the life and death of her parents an intricate reflection upon the sacramental life of the Church and the depth and breadth of Catholic faith and spirituality. The author's mastery of the Church's liturgical theology is constantly embedded within the profoundly human realities that form the sacramental nature of our life on this earth.

Most Reverend Robert W. Bishop of San Diego

Keep at It, Riley!

To Tim,

Thank you for all your excellent work to promote Catholic Liturgy. Your presence and catechesis through your teaching and writing is a tremendous blessing to many. Keep at it, Riley!

Peace,
Noreen

Keep at It, Riley!

Accompanying my Father
through Death into Life

Noreeh Madden McInnes

New City Press
Hyde Park, New York

Published by New City Press
202 Comforter Blvd.,
Hyde Park, NY 12538
www.newcitypress.com

Keep at It, Riley!
Accompanying my Father through Death into Life

Noreen Madden McInnes

Cover design and layout by Miguel Tejerina

Library of Congress Control Number: 2022902504

ISBN: 978-1-56548-526-6 (Paperback)
ISBN: 978-1-56548-532-7 (E-book)

Printed in the United States of America

Contents

Series Preface

Does the book that you are about to read seem unusual? Perhaps even counterintuitive?

Good. The Magenta series wouldn't be doing its job if you felt otherwise.

On the color wheel, magenta lies directly between red and blue. Just so, books in this series do not lie at one limit or another of our hopelessly simplistic, two-dimensional, antagonistic, binary imagination. Often, in the broader culture any answer to a moral or political question gets labeled as liberal or conservative, red or blue. But the Magenta series refuses to play by these shortsighted rules. Magenta will address the complexity of the issues of our day by resisting a framework that unnecessarily pits one idea against another. Magenta refuses to be defined by anything other than a positive vision of the good.

If you understand anything about the Focolare's dialogical-and-faithful mission, it should not surprise you that this series has found a home with the Focolare's New City Press. The ideas in these books, we believe, will spark dialogues that will heal divides and build unity at the very sites of greatest fragmentation and division.

The ideas in Magenta are crucial not only for our fragmented culture, but also for the Church. Our secular idolatry— our simplistic left/right, red/blue imagination— has oozed into the Church as well, disfiguring the Body of

Christ with ugly disunity. Such idolatry, it must be said, has muffled the Gospel and crippled the Church, keeping it from being salt and light in a wounded world desperate for unity.

Magenta is not naïve. We realize full well that appealing to dialogue or common ground can be dismissed as a weak-sauce, milquetoast attempt to cloud our vision of the good or reduce it to a mere least common denominator. We know that much dialogic spade work is yet to be done, but that does not keep the vision of the Magenta Series (like the color it bears) from being *bold*. There is nothing half-hearted about it. All our authors have a brilliant, attractive vision of the good.

I think you'll find that Noreen McInnes's *Keep at It Riley!* will be a paradigmatic example of such a vision in our series. Mostly by masterful, heartfelt, and deeply moving storytelling, her book builds an essential foundation for the kind of human dignity promoted by the series by illustrating what it means to accompany a family member through their final stages of life. Can I get away with saying "you'll laugh and you'll cry" several times as you read this book? Because you will. And even more importantly, the foundation of your faith in God and humanity will be profoundly strengthened. Something, I suspect, many of us could use these days.

Enjoy!
Charles C. Camosy

Acknowledgments

I am thankful for being truly blessed with wonderful parents, Frank and Joan Madden, and all my family before them, especially for handing down their Irish Catholic faith. I am profoundly grateful for my children: Greg, Kelley, and Mollie, daughter-in-law: Christina, grandchildren: Connor and Ellie, sisters: Mari and Ellyn, brothers-in-law: Jim and Andy, nieces: Aileen, Haley, and Riley, all my cousins, and the Mountain Top community for their loving support. I would like to express my deep gratitude for all of Frank's caregivers that made his time in our home possible, in particular: Brian Birdsong, Reynaldo Caguitla, and Sergio Garcia.

I offer my sincere appreciation to all who have helped me in the writing and publication of this book: to those who read the manuscript and added their own unique bits of wisdom: Mary Backer, Chris Berg, Rev. Mark Campbell, Julie Dolnik, Rev. Michael Driscoll, Sean Embury, Mary Ann Fallon, Deacon Scott Frampton, Carole Hoffmann, Julie Igel, Joan McDonald, Marycarol Reeder NP, Bridget Rohmiller, Emily Rotunda, Dr. Sherry Rotunda, Carol Tunney, and Sr. Kathleen Warren, OSF; to New City Press for their support, in particular, Tom Masters for his patient editing; and especially to Charlie Camosy for his invitation and vision for this book.

Finally, and most importantly, yet it's not possible to fully express in words how grateful I am for my husband Peter, *mo anam cara*, for his constant love and support. None of this would have happened without him.

Introduction

I t was a mistake. I should not have been the one that was called to help my aging parents as their lives slowly unraveled. They needed someone with medical knowledge to help them address their numerous and complex health issues; my younger sister, Ellyn, the nurse, would have been the obvious choice. They needed someone with legal expertise to organize their estate; my older sister, Mari, the lawyer, would have been perfect. They also needed a cook and a housekeeper; pretty much anyone else on the planet would have been a better choice for that than me. Why was I called? I am just a choir director, a liturgist, and a student of theology, I didn't have any of the necessary skills to reach out to my parents at this time of their lives. Or did I?

Thinking that I was following the will of God, I had planned a missionary trip to Burundi, but it became clear that it was only my plan, not God's. I was called to be a missionary not to Africa, but to Pennsylvania. Though I had my doubts, I said "yes." I took a leap of faith and committed to do whatever I could, with the help of God. "Let it be done to me according to your Word" (Lk 1:38).[1]

My husband and I had left Pennsylvania for California thirty years ago, full of adventure, taking a chance on a life far away from family and friends. But every summer we would pack up our three kids and the dog and head back

East for what I jokingly called the "inheritance tour." Now, I would be crisscrossing the country on a ministry tour—to my sick and aging parents.

This is a story about how Catholic faith accompanied my family through the sickness and death of my elderly parents. What could mistakenly be described as a downward spiral, was instead, graciously upwards. As my parents were called home to God those around them caught a glimpse of heaven. Ministering to them during this time was challenging, but not a burden. It was a tremendous blessing and a profound witness to the teaching of St. Francis, that in giving, we receive.

Our aging, sick, and dying need more than medical knowledge and legal expertise; they and their loved ones are often thirsting for spiritual care. Ministry to the sick is an extension of the mission of Jesus who cared for the whole person, body and soul, as he "went around to all the towns and villages, teaching in their synagogues, proclaiming the gospel of the kingdom, and curing every disease and illness" (Mt 9:35). Today the Catholic Church continues to bring the healing touch of Christ to the infirm and the marginalized through the sacraments for Pastoral Care of the Sick: Communion of the Sick, Anointing of the Sick, and Viaticum.[2] And when we are called home to God, the celebration of the Order of Christian Funerals comforts those mourning with hope in the resurrection and in thanksgiving for the gift of a life now returned to God.

I came to realize that I had everything I needed to answer the call. I discovered my source of strength was my Irish Catholic upbringing, the sacraments, and my God. Our family motto, "Keep at it Riley!" sums it up well. We don't give up; we never quit; we give it to God. These priceless treasures I had inherited from my parents. Now I hope to pass them down to generations to come, and to you, dear reader.

Sucipe

Take, Lord, and receive
all my liberty,
my memory,
my understanding,
and my entire will -
all that I have and call my own.
You have given it all to me.
To you, Lord, I return it.
Everything is yours;
do with it what you will.
Give me only your love and your grace.
That is enough for me.

St. Ignatius of Loyola

Chapter 1

Can We Be Your Africa?

I called my father, Frank, just as I had many times before, waiting nervously for the phone to be picked up, hoping to hear his voice, hoping he was still alive and well for one more day.

"Hello!"

Sigh, he's there, thanks be to God. I read so much into that one word, "Hello." Is his voice weak? How's his breathing? Was that a little wheeze I heard? You'd think that his "Hello" was worth a hundred lab tests. I'm in California, far away from my aging parents in Mountain Top, Pennsylvania, the little town where I grew up, so I have to depend on my "Telephonic Medical Diagnostic System."

"Hi, Dad. How are you today?"

"Hi, Noreen. I'm doing pretty good. What's new?"

"Well, I am planning a trip to Africa."

"Oh, wow! Africa. Why Africa?"

"A friend of mine is going on a missionary trip to Burundi, and she asked me to come along."

"What are you going to do there?"

"I don't really know—but I'll do whatever is needed: English lessons, prison ministry, music ministry. . ."

"How long would you go for?"

"At least two weeks."

"Oh! hmmm. . ."

As I explained Africa to my father, I could almost hear the wheels turning in his head. One question slowly followed the other, and then finally, there it was:

"Can *we* be your Africa?"

The world stopped for just a second. My life would never be the same again. My father's irresistible charm and his skills as a lifelong fisherman had me on the hook before I even saw it coming. I heard myself respond, "Of course, you can be my Africa." Little did I know that the "African journey" that I was about to begin would take me much further and deeper than the one I had originally planned. It wasn't the "sexy" missionary trip I'd dreamed about. No, it was far better; it was work that had *my* name on it. I heard *my* name called, "Come, follow me." I left my nets behind and followed Him.

Frank, at eighty years of age, had a mind as sharp as a tack but his body, not so much. He couldn't get around the way he used to. He was suffering from the usual suspects: Chronic Obstructive Pulmonary Disease (COPD), Congestive Heart Failure (CHF), arthritis, diabetes, and neuropathy. Joan, his bride of fifty-eight years, was quite spry and got around just fine; she just couldn't always remember where she was going. But Frank and Joan made a great team. Together they could take on the world—one could move and the other could navigate. Separately, though, they struggled. The life they were holding onto was unraveling.

The typical day in Mountain Top started early. Mom hit the floor running, scurrying about making Frank his usual breakfast of oatmeal and coffee, throwing in a load of laundry, and then dashing off to morning Mass at St. Jude's. She would be sure to leave the front door unlocked in case emergency medical technicians needed to rush Frank to the hospital as they had several times before. Frank had fallen into a daunting cycle: water retention, fever, struggling to breathe, ambulance, hospital, rehab facility, back home, then repeat. Mom had notebooks full of daily weigh-ins and medication lists. As a retired high school math teacher, she was fond of data collection and statistical analysis. She could sniff out the warning signs of a bad trend long before any blood test or diagnostic imaging. She was his pharmacist, advocate, chef, laundress, and prayer warrior. But what she did best was being his cheerleader.

Mom never lost her optimism; she was convinced that everything was going to get better. Mom would return home from Mass renewed, filled with all the grace she needed to take on the day. Like clockwork, mom would walk in the door and go right to Frank, to check on him and let him know "I prayed for you this morning at Mass."

Frank, always grateful for the prayers, replied, "That's good. Thank you, dear."

On his good days, Frank would be stationed at his command center, holding court at the kitchen table. Everything to govern his universe was within arm's reach. Frank might struggle to walk unassisted, but with his phone and his charm he could reach the ends of the earth.

They enjoyed the rhythm of their life and were content to continue this way forever. Most days they were even convinced they could. You see, Frank never gave up on anything, an instinct that was implanted from the early days of his youth. As a child, the phrase, "Keep at it, Riley!" which felt like a curse cast upon him, became his gift.

From the time Frank and his sister, Joan Marie, were in grade school, the nightly ritual was to go up to their rooms after supper and finish their homework. As their father stopped in to check on them before bed, he'd visit

Joan Marie's room first. Frank could clearly hear his father ask her, "How are the studies going?", and she'd sheepishly reply that she had more to do. My grandfather would soothingly say, "Well that's enough for tonight, dear, it's time to turn out the lights. Say your prayers and go to bed!"

Next came the visit to Frank's room. "How are the studies going?" Expecting the same compassion, Frank admitted that he had more to do. But, as my grandfather headed out of the room, he'd spout over his shoulder, "Well, keep at it, Riley!" Night after night, those words irritated Frank to no end; he was never able to quiet the voice of his father within him, "Keep at it, Riley!" But that line became the blessing that helped him persist through enormous challenges all throughout his life.

My mother used a different approach to problems; she had the uncanny ability to see the world through rose-colored glasses. There were no problems! You don't have to acknowledge the elephant in the room if you don't look at it. Fortunately, Frank had better vision, and saw clearly that they did indeed need help. And now help was on the way. Mountain Top, here I come.

Prayer

Lord, give us the ambition
to do as much as we can,
as well as we can,
as long as we can,
and the resolve not to despair
over the things we cannot do.

Theodore M. Hesburgh, CSC

Chapter 2

Keep at It, Riley!

Growing up in a coal mining town during the Depression, Frank learned early how to leverage the little he had. Even at the age of ten, Frank earned spending money by offering to his neighbors, "For four cents I can load your bucket of cinders and ashes onto my wagon and take it out to the street for you." Though coal furnaces kept the homes toasty warm throughout the cold northeastern Pennsylvania winters, it was messy business hauling the weekly residual cinders and ashes out to the curb for pickup. Young Frank was strong, worked hard, and knew how to put his new red Christmas wagon to good use. When his business became a success, he decided to make a further offer: "For six cents, I'll carry your bucket up from your cellar and out to the curb." The neighbors had learned to count on Frank, and many were eager to take the next step. For an extra two cents they trusted him to carry the filthy ashes through the house without making a disastrous mess! Keep at it, Riley!

In the upside-down wisdom of God, what often comes disguised as a curse, in the end turns out to be a tremendous blessing. And so it was with Frank Madden. His curse wasn't as agonizing as some dread disease or nasty disfigurement; he was merely saddled with a constant reminder that Maddens don't ever give up, or give in. If anything, we work harder. And, for God's sake, Maddens *never* quit! This was part of Frank's DNA. It would prove to serve him well and indeed bless him tremendously.

I don't know how many generations of Maddens have been saying "Keep at it, Riley!" but I know they certainly lived by it. My grandfather, Jack Madden, dropped out of school in the second grade to help feed his nine brothers and sisters. His father, despite holding down three jobs, still couldn't make ends meet and ended up working himself to death. As many of the young Irish American lads did in those days, Jack took a job in the coal mines as a breaker boy. Six days a week the boys would sit on a bench perched above a conveyor belt to pick out the slate from the coal that passed beneath them. By twelve years of age, Jack graduated to coal miner and was sent down into dark, cavernous mines to shovel coal into carts. Jack, strong, strapping, and single minded, negotiated to be paid by the number of carts he could fill instead of the typical hourly rate. It served him quite well since he eventually saved enough money to earn his ticket out of the mines and open a bar perched high on a hill in Pittston, Pennsylvania.

Jack was well-liked by many, and—fortunately—that included the cops. Having the local law enforcement on your side was crucial since Prohibition was in full swing at the time, which meant that the sale of all alcoholic beverages was banned. With a wink and a nod, the officers would let Jack know that they would be stopping in for a "visit" later in the day. The tip-off on the raid put the barmen into action. Out came the barrels and down the hill they'd roll. They were quickly stashed in a safe house at the bottom of the hill until the coast was clear. After the "visit" the barmen deftly loaded the barrels onto their horse-drawn cart. My great-grandmother Katie, mother of ten and a young widow, had a pretty little smile and a big hoop skirt that coyly covered up the barrels as they made their way back up the hill.

After Jack married my grandmother, Anna McCarty, he reformed his wily ways. He left the bar and made an honest wage as an insurance salesman. Like many, in the stock market crash of 1929 Jack lost the bundle of cash he made at the bar. My grandmother, with her consistently good influence, consoled and counseled him that it was just as well. I can still hear her say, "Now Jack, it was all for the best. It was bad money anyway."

Jack was a good man, respected and honored by family and friends alike. After the banks crashed, with no safe place to deposit money, many turned to Jack to hold their cash. Without reservation, they trusted him. They knew that if anything happened to them, he would take care of their loved ones and set their affairs in order.

In a prophetic way, Jack shared with me his tremendous compassion for the aging and infirmed. My grandfather took me along with him as he made his regular rounds to visit and check on his elderly widowed sisters. But the unwavering, loving care that Jack showed for my grandmother, Anna, was dearest of all. From an early age she suffered from debilitating arthritis, and as she grew older her movement became more and more impaired. Without hesitation, Jack took on the role of her caretaker and ran the house and home with the utmost proficiency, love, and compassion.

Watching Jack behold his sisters and his wife with dignity, regardless of their frail condition, taught me a great deal about him, those he cared for, and how Christ continues his outreach to the marginalized through others today. It was the mustard seed planted within me that would germinate and open my eyes and heart to see clearly that God calls *us* to be *his* hands and *his* loving embrace to the sick, the dying, the aging, and all those in need.

Jack never complained. He never gave up! All his life he was a man for others. How did Jack "Keep at it, Riley!"? What keeps the Maddens strong? The Maddens never quit because even deeper in our DNA than "Keep at it, Riley!" is our strong faith and trust in God. The same unwavering faith that strengthened and carried the starving Maddens out of the Great Famine in Ireland to the coal mines of Pennsylvania still carries us today. Our God does not promise a life free of oppression, pain, and poverty. But our God does promise to accompany us through all our suffering and to remain with us always until the end of the age (Mt 28:20).

St. Patrick, patron saint of Ireland, credited with bringing Christianity to the Irish, taught us well. Patrick himself experienced a curse that became his blessing. Kidnapped by pirates at the age of sixteen, he was taken as a slave for six years to Ireland, where he endured great loneliness and hardship. Through that time of darkness, Patrick turned to prayer and comfort in the Lord that nurtured a deep faith. After escaping from captivity, in abundant gratitude for the gift of his faith, he felt called to return to Ireland to preach the Gospel to the pagan country. In his *Confession*, Patrick described his vocation in his own words:

> There's no way then, that I'm going to keep quiet about this – for what good would that do? I mean keep quiet about how the Lord favoured me with all sorts of graces and blessings, in this land where once I was a slave. For that is how we pay our dues to God after he has corrected us, and we have taken it to heart: we show how glad we are by shouting out the marvellous things he's done, so that every nation under the sun can hear about them.[3]

Patrick spent the remainder of his days in Ireland, tirelessly baptizing and evangelizing. And as Patrick taught the Irish to look at the shamrock and see a symbol of the Trinity, three persons in one God, Jack taught me to look at the sick and see the face of God.

The Maddens don't give up. When we arise each day, we put on the Breastplate of St. Patrick. As we pray St. Patrick's prayer, we acknowledge that on our own we are nothing, but with the God of our ancestors, we have a mighty strength.

Breastplate of St. Patrick

I arise today
through God's strength to pilot me;
God's might to uphold me,
God's wisdom to guide me,
God's eye to look before me,
God's ear to hear me,
God's word to speak for me,
God's hand to guard me,
God's way to lie before me,
God's shield to protect me,
God's hosts to save me
From snares of the devil,
From temptations of vices,
From every one who shall wish me ill,
Afar and anear. . .
Christ with me, Christ before me, Christ behind me,
Christ in me, Christ beneath me, Christ above me,
Christ on my right, Christ on my left,
Christ when I lie down, Christ when I sit down,
Christ in the heart of every one who thinks of me,
Christ in the mouth of every one who speaks of me,
Christ in every eye that sees me,
Christ in every ear that hears me.

I arise today
Through a mighty strength, the invocation of the Trinity,
Through a belief in the Threeness,
Through a confession of the Oneness
Of the Creator of creation.

Chapter 3

When the Angels Came

Mom Conway, 91 years young and Noreen, 2 years old.

Everyone called her "Mom"—her ten children, her grandchildren, and even me, one of her dozens of great-grandchildren. All her neighbors and friends knew my maternal great-grandmother as "Mom Conway." She was everyone's mom; she had enough love to go around for all of us. On Sundays, her house was always overflowing with family and friends. Everyone stopped in for a bite, a laugh, and a jar. A jar? That's what Mom Conway called her glass or her pint, just as we sing it out loud and proud in the Irish song, "Wack fall the daddy-o, there's whiskey in the jar."

During the Spanish flu, the pandemic of 1918, Mom Conway spent her days going from home to home, unafraid of getting sick herself. She doled out her special home remedies to cure whatever ailed you. She whipped together a potion of honey, lemon, and white-of-the-egg to soothe a sore throat or a tickly cough. For chest congestion she made you a mustard plaster, a paste of dry mustard, flour, and water, spread between two rags. She would pin it under your shirt, so it would lie directly on your chest. The paste would soon start to warm up, turning your skin red, and sending vapors of the mustard wafting in through your nostrils. The lucky ones would get a hot toddy, a few drops of whiskey in warm sweetened tea. But the best home remedy was the one Mom Conway had waiting when she finally made her way home. She claimed it was that shot of Jameson each night that kept her from coming down with the Spanish flu herself.

When Mom Conway reached her advanced years, Nana, my maternal grandmother, invited her to move into her home, just as Mom Conway had welcomed her own mother. It wasn't ideal for any of them, since Mom Conway had to share a room with my mother and my aunt during their teenaged years. But my mom and my aunt never complained, especially since she always covered for them whenever they snuck in late at night after curfew.

I have fond memories of snuggling with Mom Conway in Nana's kitchen, snapping green beans and singing songs. But one day, just after I turned three, I clearly remember running up the steep steps in Nana's house to the second floor, looking for Mom Conway. She wasn't downstairs and I thought she might be up in her bedroom. My godfather, Uncle Jim, who lived there too, gently caught me at the top of the steps. Puzzled, I asked, "Where's Mom?"

He tenderly smiled, pointed upwards, and said "The angels came and took her up to heaven." At three I couldn't really process whether that was a good thing or a bad thing, but I understood that was the way it was. And, to this day, that's how I understand death. The angels will come and take us up to heaven. Even though we don't know the day or the hour, we need not be afraid.

Mom Conway was our most Irish relative. She was born in Ireland; she still had the Irish brogue and sang all the old songs. When Notre Dame football games were broadcast on the radio, she'd settle into her rocking chair, her white wispy hair swept up in a bun and her black hand-knitted shawl tightly wrapped around her shoulders. She'd deliberately rock her chair and get her rosary beads going, praying for the Fighting Irish to bring home another win. Go Irish!

As I started researching my genealogy, I wasn't surprised to find Mom Conway's death certificate, filled out by Uncle Jim, documenting that she was born in County Mayo, Ireland and lived a long life of ninety-two years. But I was startled by what I learned from the census records. I discovered that Mom Conway's parents, Mary Sullivan, of County Kerry, and John Healey, of County Sligo, were born in Ireland. Around 1850, Mary and John joined the one million Irish refugees fleeing the Great Famine. Another million less fortunate Irish died of starvation or related illnesses. Mary and John fled to England where they married in 1855 and had six children, one of whom was my Mom Conway. At the age of sixteen she emigrated from England to Pennsylvania and three years later, became a naturalized United States citizen. Mom Conway never set foot in Ireland!

Why say that you were born in Ireland, not England? Could it be that living in England doesn't make you English? Can you claim your family's country of origin and deny the country you reside in if you retain your culture and language? Or did Mom Conway deny England because of the resentment that still runs deep in the veins of the Irish who blame the English for the Great Famine?

The mass starvation was caused by a terrible blight that destroyed a staple crop on which the Irish depended, the lumper. Though the English didn't cause the blight, they did deny sufficient aid or a path to survival. Since the 1801 Act of Union left Irish Catholics without representation in Parliament, Ireland had effectively been a colony of England. Under this rule and the Penal Laws, Catholics, eighty percent of the Irish at the time, were prohibited from owning or leasing land, voting, holding office, getting an education, and owning firearms. Mostly absentee English landlords demanded rent for property that could no longer produce the potatoes which for many provided the sole source of income and food. Unable to pay the rent, the Irish were evicted and quickly became both hungry and homeless, wandering about and sleeping in ditches.

While the Irish starved, the absentee landlords continued to export oats, corn, and livestock from Ireland to England. In a weak attempt to save lives, England imported a meager amount of American maize to the Irish markets. That policy failed since maize didn't have the nutritional value of the potato, was in short supply, and needed to be milled to make it edible. Since there were very few mills, the desperate and starving became seriously ill eating unprocessed maize. The lack of adequate food and nutrition weakened immune systems. The Irish that didn't die of starvation were vulnerable to diseases caused by malnutrition. Several successive years of crop failure and sickness left the Irish in a severely depressed physical and mental state. Those caught stealing food, even out of desperation, were sent on prison ships to Australia, leaving many with only two options: death, or emigration.

In addition to the physical maladies, decades without education ensured the Irish Catholics' disadvantage to rise above their oppression. At the time of the Great Famine fewer than half of the population in Ireland were literate. Jack Madden's grandfather left during the famine and census records show that he arrived in Pennsylvania unable to read or write. Since mining didn't require literacy, only strength of mind and body, many Irish worked in the mines to put food on the table. It wasn't until two generations later that the Maddens were able to escape the dangers of the mines for a better life.

Death and dismemberment were no strangers to mine workers. The breaker boys, precariously perched above a conveyor belt full of moving coal, would often slip and fall into the machinery, losing fingers, arms, or even their lives. Those that went down into the mines risked dying in a collapsed shaft or by asphyxiation. Only a fortunate few had a canary in the coal mine.

Everyone feared the notorious Black Maria, a horse-drawn cart that carried the dead home from the mines, heartlessly leaving the body lying across the front porch. Having a strong faith and trust in the Lord was the only way families could bear this pain. They took comfort knowing that the angels came and took their loved ones up to heaven. Perhaps that is why many Irish have a devotion to praying the Angelus, which recalls a momentous occasion when an angel came to earth. The Angelus, Latin for angel, recounts the Angel Gabriel announcing to Mary the incarnation, the coming of Christ in the fullness of time to dwell among us in human flesh. Beginning in the thirteenth century Angelus bells have called the faithful to prayer and continue to do so in some places today. Bells toll at six in the morning, noon, and six in the evening with three sets of three peals, followed by nine more. The prayer reminds us that in all things we have hope; that God is with us, Emmanuel. Jesus was sent to "bring good news to the oppressed, to bind up the broken-hearted" (Is 61:1).

The Angelus Prayer, painted by Jean-Francois Millet around 1850, depicts French peasant potato farmers suspending their work to pray the Angelus. You can almost hear the church bells ringing from the across the field calling them to prayer during the days when the potato farmers in Ireland were starving to death.

My father, Frank, fondly remembered his mother taking him into town as a young boy to meet her three maiden sisters, Mary, Margaret, and Teresa, at St. Mary's, the Irish church, to pray the Angelus together at noon. The Angelus bells still ring on Irish radio and television today, the same call to prayer that reverberated through generations of our ancestors. The Angelus prayer affirms faith in the resurrection and the hope for admittance to the heavenly kingdom where every tear will be wiped away.[4]

The Angelus by Jean Francois Millet

The Angelus

V. The Angel of the Lord declared unto Mary.
R. And she conceived of the Holy Spirit.
Hail, Mary, full of grace, the Lord is with thee. Blessed art thou among women, and blessed is the fruit of thy womb, Jesus. Holy Mary, Mother of God, pray for us sinners, now and at the hour of our death. Amen.

V. Behold the handmaid of the Lord.
R. Be it done unto me according to thy word.
Hail, Mary. . .

V. And the Word was made flesh.
R. And dwelt among us.
Hail, Mary. . .

V. Pray for us, O Holy Mother of God.
R. That we may be made worthy
of the promises of Christ.

Let us pray.
Pour forth, we beseech Thee, O Lord,
thy grace into our hearts;
that we, to whom the incarnation of Christ, thy Son,
was made known by the message of an angel,
may by his Passion and Cross be brought
to the glory of his Resurrection,
through the same Christ Our Lord. Amen.

m

Chapter 4

Mountain Top

Many would describe Mountain Top, in north-eastern Pennsylvania, as God's country. Is that because of the elevation? Well, no. Mountain Top, only 1,558 feet above sea level, isn't on much of a mountain. But it stands higher than all the rolling mountains around and marks a ridge that divides the watershed down to the Susquehanna River basin to the north and west, and to the Lehigh River basin to the east and south. It began as a town of modest means built beside a railyard to house railroad employees and those that worked in the nearby mines. Yet, its natural beauty and inexpensive land provided the perfect setting to draw growing businesses and young families with promising futures.

Mountain Top. Could you pick a more charming name? You're probably thinking of a quaint mountain village straight out of *The Sound of Music*, with Julie Andrews swinging her arms, singing "the hills are alive. . . " Mountain Top definitely does have charm, more than you could ever imagine. But you won't find cute Tyrolean chalets, flowering window boxes, or little tasty tucked-away bistros. What's the secret? Is it the fresh air, "the mountain breeze," as we called it? Is it the unveiled grandeur of God glimpsed in our snow frosted mountains as Plunkett so poetically described: "His *body gleams amid eternal snows*"? Or maybe it's the untouched forests blanketing rolling hills that become an explosion of color in autumn calling back every heart that has ever strayed? No, the charm you'll find is hidden in the hearts of the most loving people you will ever know.

Without question, the secret for the special love found in Mountain Top is St. Jude's Catholic Church. Who knew that painted cinder blocks in the shape of an "L" could be the crucible for deep faith and a love that binds together such a tight knit community? The families that gathered within these unpretentious walls every Sunday morning formed unbreakable bonds and received a source of strength that would endure the test of time. We made friends we could count on all our lives.

In the 1950s young families just starting out moved to Mountain Top with hopes and dreams of bright beginnings. St. Jude's Church is where they met and became family. It didn't take long before Saturday night was just as much a part of the ritual as Sunday morning! But no matter how late or raucous those Saturday night parties got, the next morning we would all be at church, showered, teeth brushed, dresses on, hair combed, bows on our heads, and ready for Mass.

All the babies were baptized in the same font, becoming adopted children of God, binding us all together as brothers and sisters in Christ. All the children knelt at the same altar railing for their First Holy Communion with an excitement of finally being able to share in the heavenly food our parents and older siblings savored. All the pre-teens processed timidly down the same aisle for Confirmation, to become fully initiated Christians. Since we were in such a rural hamlet, the bishop came only once every three years, confirming large batches of sixth, seventh, and eighth graders, all together. We swapped mothers and fathers to be our sponsors for the sacrament that strengthened the gift of the Holy Spirit we received in baptism.

During one of the Confirmation visits by the bishop, our pastor, Fr. Nolan, asked Frank for his help. There happened to be a new school gymnasium on the church campus that Fr. Nolan "forgot" to mention to the bishop. The beloved pastor could have been in deep trouble for constructing a building that size without asking for the bishop's blessing. Frank was tasked to assemble a wall of men in the church parking lot to shield the new building from the bishop's view as he walked to his car from the church. Frank would do anything for Fr. Nolan, who he fondly called "Sonny," and successfully pulled off the human screen for the good pastor.

At St. Jude's we encountered God in the sacraments and in one another. We were surrounded and formed by our faith and love in our parish family, the mystical body of Christ. You could easily imagine that it was not in Lake Wobegon but in Mountain Top, where *"all the women are strong, all the men are good looking, and all the children are above average."* But you would have to add, *"and they all went to St. Jude's, the patron saint of hopeless cases."*

For many of us "The Park" was our first Mountain Top neighborhood, which sounds like a place with stands of trees, flowerbeds, and ponds with ducks. But it didn't have any of that. It was nothing more than row houses with clotheslines intersecting the yards and walls so thin you could hear the neighbors' every move. We all knew when it was bath time at the Foley's. From an early age those five wild Foley boys were lovingly dubbed, the "Five Holy Boys."

The Park was the kind of place where our moms, in curlers and headscarves, yakked away while hanging out the wash on the clothesline; where kids, gathering to play hide and seek, used a rhyme to see who was "it":

My mother and your mother were hanging out clothes.
My mother punched your mother in the nose.
What color was the blood?
Green!
G - r - e -e - n !
and you are IT!

It is true that our moms had neither clothes dryers nor hair dryers. The kids didn't have video games, only balls, jump ropes, and hide and seek. Our black and white TV could pick up only two channels and each family had only one car. It was not true, though, that our moms punched each other; they were a tight knit family that supported each other through good times and bad.

All the children went to St. Jude's Catholic Elementary School, with two classes per grade. My grade was always the biggest, with one hundred students split into two classes of fifty. There were no disciplinary issues. The Sisters of Christian Charity ran the school with an iron fist; we all behaved and did our work. There was no back talk and no excuses. We attended Mass every week, filing into church down the center aisle in two straight lines. The holy sisters used a clicker to choreograph our every move. One click signaled where we should stop in the aisle. The second click meant drop to your right knee, and on the third, we rose back up in unison. The fourth click meant we were to enter the pews. We moved with precision and no dissension among the ranks.

In those days the church was in transition due to the liturgical renewal of the Second Vatican Council. Prior to this time only the ordained could proclaim the Word of God at Mass. Frank was honored to be the very first lay person to be a lector at St. Jude's Church. It was a privilege that he cherished. Another change that Frank enjoyed, and possibly appreciated even more, was eating meat on Fridays. Catholics, commonly known as fish-eaters, had to abstain from meat on Fridays throughout the whole year, not just during Lent. But post Vatican II, Frank could now look forward to his Friday night hamburger.

After eighth grade, along with many of my St. Jude's classmates, I went on to Bishop Hoban Catholic High School in Wilkes-Barre. Though my mother taught math at Crestwood High School in Mountain Top, my parents thought it was important for their daughters to attend a Catholic school, which meant a longer commute. We didn't have to walk uphill both ways but, we did risk our lives winding our way down the mountain to the valley below on roads covered in ice and snow, riding in a recklessly speeding school bus without seat belts.

On the surface our childhood may have seemed idyllic, yet underneath, like everyone else's, it was not perfect. After I finished college my father's drinking and my mother's rose-colored glasses made it easy for me take a chance on a different life in California.

I See His Blood Upon the Rose

I see his blood upon the rose
And in the stars the glory of his eyes,
His body gleams amid eternal snows,
His tears fall from the skies.
I see his face in every flower;
The thunder and the singing of the birds
Are but his voice-and carven by his power
Rocks are his written words.
All pathways by his feet are worn,
His strong heart stirs the ever-beating sea,
His crown of thorns is twined with every thorn,
His cross is every tree.

Joseph Mary Plunkett

35

Chapter 5

Ministering in Mountain Top

I n response to my father's plea "Could we be your Africa?" I began traveling from California to Mountain Top every other month. I looked forward to helping my parents in this time of their lives, but I had to put aside some of the baggage I carried from my childhood. Every family is dysfunctional —except for the Holy Family, and we certainly weren't them. I needed to forgive my father for the times he preferred drinking in the bars to being at home with his wife and children and accept that my mother coped by looking the other way. No doubt, they had to forgive me for not being the perfect child. As an adult, I was able to see that we all have our faults and I learned to let it go.

At first, I couldn't accomplish very much. I was the hospitality minister, the laughing, eating, drinking, "just show up" and "be" minister. My mother, in denial as usual, was convinced that they didn't need any help. She wanted to wait on me. She wanted to tell me what to do, and certainly had no interest in taking any advice or assistance from me.

I'd ask, "Mom, can I throw in some laundry for you?"

"No, Noreen, it needs special attention."

"Mom, let me clean out the refrigerator for you while I'm home."

"No. Everything that's in the fridge is fine. There is nothing to clean out."

The refrigerator hadn't been purged in years. The five-year-old mayo could kill you, but I would get soundly scolded if I was caught tossing something out. I surrendered hopes of assisting them with chores and morphed into becoming their cruise director.

A treasured part of the trip to Mountain Top was accompanying mom to morning Mass at St. Jude's. We would arrive fifteen minutes early so she could settle into her pew where she had worn in her kneeler from her daily devotions. I would kneel beside her as she prayed the novena to St. Jude, patron saint of the impossible, for my dad. I could finally see that her faith was her rose colored glasses. It wasn't that she didn't recognize she had problems or lived in complete denial; she had a steadfast faith, hope, and trust in the Lord that ensured all shall be well.

After the twenty-minute Mass, mom would make her rounds. She would first check on "her" candle, in front of the statue of St. Jude, symbolizing her constant prayers for his intercession. She would visit her "friends," stopping before the statues of Padre Pio, the Sacred Heart of Jesus, and St. Thérèse of Lisieux to make a request and get a word of advice. A special moment in front of the Pietà always evoked a comment that she wanted a holy death; she wanted to go to Mass on Sunday and be buried by Saturday. I honestly did not pay much attention, since her mother, my Nana, and her grandmother, Mom Conway, both lived to be ninety-two. So, that meant she had a good ten years left and with today's health care advances probably even more.

During those visits to Mountain Top, while my father was in the hospital, I would take mom out to breakfast after Mass to the local classic small-town diner. As you crossed the threshold you took a quick scan of the room to see if there was anyone you didn't know. After breakfast we would spend the day with my father in the hospital, where mom would stay faithfully by his side, alternating between praying the rosary and working at Sudoku. At the end of the long day, I would take her out to Cavanaugh's for some healthy food, a cocktail, and many friendly faces. Cavanaugh's, the "Cheers" of Mountain Top, was the pub where everyone knows your name, your family, and all your business. Since the Foleys owned it, you could count on at least one of them presiding from a nearby bar stool. And, since Mrs. Foley's maiden name was Cavanaugh and the bar was named for her, it practically felt like we were in her living room.

The Foley family had treasured my mom ever since she came racing to their home to pray with the boys after their father had suddenly passed away. Even though that happened more than thirty years ago and the youngest was only in kindergarten at the time, they never forgot praying the Our Father, Hail Mary, and Glory Be, on their knees, with my mother for their dad.

At Cavanaugh's I would buy a round of our usual cocktails, a gin and tonic for mom, a CC and ginger for Mrs. Foley, and a Yuengling for me. A few sips into the adult beverages I would try to get some advice on child rearing from Mrs. Foley. Having raised five boys on her own, she was a pillar of strength and wisdom. It was clear that what sustained her was not human but divine. I often wondered how she survived the many challenging scrapes and mischief her boys were famous for. I would ask her how she managed, and she would reply with a twinkle in her eye, "I don't know what you are talking about. I always knew where my sons were; they were either in the library or in the church."

There was no one in Cavanaugh's that didn't know mom. As the local high school math teacher, she had either taught them or their children or both. She had the reputation of being the mountain's best math teacher. Her students not only learned math, but each had a special place in her heart and they all knew it. Everyone took delight in chatting with mom. As soon as dinner was finished, she was always eager to "work the room" and visit with all her students. As the night came to a close and I asked for the check, mom was careful to point out discreetly when the addition on a bill needed to be double-checked.

I started to suspect that mom was struggling to cook. Whether it was due to exhaustion or confusion, the end was the same. Then, one night the confirmation came that mom was no longer preparing meals from scratch. Frank had just come home from the hospital and I wanted to make him a home cooked meal. So I turned on the oven to preheat and within minutes smoke started pouring out. I peeked in only to find that it was jammed full of boxes of oatmeal, Triscuits, saltines, and empty take-out containers. Worried that I couldn't get my dad out of the house, I called the fire department right away. Within minutes, three of the hottest guys in Mountain Top, dressed in firefighter gear, stormed into the kitchen and took charge of the situation. Of course, we already knew them and all their family. I was relieved to know such an impressive team was close by to help us in an emergency— or to liven up an otherwise dull evening.

My sisters and I worried that mom was slipping. But at what point do you intervene? Aren't we all slipping in some way? If mom asked me the same question repeatedly, I would just answer as if it were the first time she'd asked. What good would it do to point out that I already answered the question? She obviously didn't remember. If she told me the same story for the tenth time, I could still nod and patiently enjoy the story once again. While it is a red flag, it isn't a stop sign. There is a difference. But it was something to keep my eye on. She received countless phone calls and letters from "religious" organizations. Could any of them be charading as holy missionaries in order to swindle mom out of some significant money? More importantly, when dad was home should mom still be in charge of giving him his meds? She would never give that up without a fight.

The best Mountain Top days were when Frank was out of the hospital and back home at his command center. Yet he wouldn't admit that he was struggling to walk and he refused to use a cane or a walker. He even turned down my best sales pitch. I was certain that I could tempt him with an Irish shillelagh, a walking stick made of knotty Blackthorn wood imported from the Emerald Isle. I was sure he'd give in when I told him that our ancestors in the old country probably used one to make their way home from the pub each night. Though I struck out on the shillelagh, I was able to convince Frank that using a walker wasn't a life sentence. I told him, "You have good days and bad days, and you'll only need to use the walker on the bad days." That worked for him, and he finally agreed. He found that being able to live his life more fully outweighed the embarrassment of needing a walker. In fact, it worked so well, the walker soon gave way to a scooter.

Frank's very first trip with his new scooter may come as a shock. It wasn't to The Alberdeen Inn, his favorite Mountain Top restaurant, or to a basketball game at King's College, his alma mater. It was for a missionary trip to the local prison. Frank went to visit Charlie, a co-worker for many years at the insurance company. Frank had listened to him complain, year after year, that his wife had been verbally abusing him from morning to night. He was a beaten man. Frank lent a sympathetic ear to Charlie's plight for so long that he wasn't surprised when Charlie just couldn't take it anymore. But many others were totally stunned and appalled when they heard that Charlie, the nice guy in the office, one day did the unthinkable. He murdered his wife and his son. Immediately after Charlie shot them, he called the police to report what he had done. In a surreal way, Charlie waited on the front porch for the police to arrive and haul him off to prison. He didn't put up a fight; he simply waived a defense attorney and pled guilty. Though my sisters and I reminded Frank that Charlie could have, and certainly should have, walked away instead of murdering his family, Frank had utmost compassion and wrote letters to him frequently. And now with the scooter he could also visit him in jail. Frank showed us in a compelling way how to love the sinner but hate the sin and he reminded us that one of the seven corporal works of mercy is to visit the imprisoned, not to judge them.

Since the scooter allowed Frank to get around faster and expend less energy, he soon resumed some of the things he enjoyed in life. One of his favorite chores was grocery shopping. It got him out of the house, but more importantly, he could buy all the food he liked. Frank would drive down the mountain to a grocery store that had a "Helping Hands" program. He would park his van, get on his scooter, and be paired up with a young man to escort him around the vast store to help him with the shopping. The youth would reach for the items on the shelves, fill up a grocery basket, help Frank through the check-out, and lastly load the purchases into the van. By the end of the shopping spree, Frank would know all about the young man, his hobbies, his family, and his plans for life. And surprisingly, Frank often knew more about the boy's family history than he did.

Frank would start slowly, "What's your name, son?"

"Thomas O'Boyle"

Then he tried to pinpoint the family, "So, are you the O'Boyles from South Wilkes-Barre or the ones from down in Plymouth?"

"My family lives in South Wilkes-Barre now, but my grandparents used to live in Plymouth."

Frank surprised him with the inside scoop, "Oh, yeah. I knew your grandparents, James, and Mary, really well. Did you know your grandmother made the best mincemeat pies in all of Wyoming Valley? Before Christmas, I would stop in, and she would have a couple of pies waiting for me."

"I never knew that she made mincemeat pies. I am sorry to say I didn't even know her that well. She died when I was only five years old."

Frank always wrapped it up encouraging him to go on to college, make a good life for himself, and be the very best that he could be. Maybe the store thought the helping hands were those of the young man, but I suspect Frank had helping hands as well.

Because of the scooter, Frank was able to continue something else that he loved—swimming. He enjoyed an aqua therapy program for arthritis sufferers at a local rehab center, but the pool was quite a distance from the parking lot. With the scooter, he wouldn't be worn out even before he got into the water. The pool, heated up to a balmy ninety degrees, had a lift chair to lower Frank gently into the soothing waters from the deck. The weightless workout did wonders for his arthritic joints. What seemed to be the best medicine, though, was the companionship of the other swimmers, each of whom suffered from varying degrees of arthritis-related disabilities. Frank encouraged them to become a support group for one another and organized regular lunches and even started an annual Christmas Party. If the flu season had to push the Christmas party back to March or April, Frank would still work to make it happen. Keep at it, Riley!

One of the highlights of Frank's routine was a monthly lunch with his men's group from St. Jude's. Their tight-knit relationship solidified when they made a Cursillo retreat weekend together decades ago and over the years deepened through their monthly prayer meetings. Madden, Costigan, Orloski, DeRojas, Balz, and Rodeway were a close group that supported each other in their Catholic faith and service to the church. They volunteered in various ways: reading at Mass, singing in the choir, or taking Holy Communion to the homebound. But they all looked forward to working at St. Jude's annual picnic. One of their favorite jobs during the picnic was selling raffle tickets for a chance to win a brand-new car. Their ticket booth was always lively and enjoyed record sales every year. I wonder if the pitcher of Manhattans that Fr. Mullen always dropped off had anything to do with their spirited success?

The walker, and then the scooter, allowed Frank to continue to attend the deeply gratifying lunches with the men's group. Their mutual love, prayer, and communion helped them through the many ups and downs of their lives and spilled over to their wives and children. As they advanced in years, their fellowship became an even more cherished bond.

When Frank began to decline further and became homebound, my mother would call St. Jude's to request that Holy Communion be brought to him. Joe Balz, one of the men's lunch group and our longtime friend, was also the homebound minister. When Joe called to say he was on his way, mom lit a white candle she had placed into a glass candlestick shaped like a crucifix awaiting the arrival of the Blessed Sacrament into her home, her husband, and her domestic church. Never having seen that candlestick before, I asked where it came from. She said that her mother had used it when Holy Communion was brought to the house for her father. Little did I know that soon I would be lighting the white candle in the candlestick when my father moved into my home.

Novena to St. Jude Thaddeus
Patron Saint of Desperate Situations and Hopeless Cases

Most holy Apostle, St. Jude, faithful servant and friend of Jesus,
the Church honors and invokes you universally,
as the patron of difficult cases, of things almost despaired of,
pray for me, I am so helpless and alone.
Intercede with God for me that He bring visible and speedy help
where help is almost despaired of.
Come to my assistance in this great need
that I may receive the consolation and help of heaven
in all my necessities, tribulations and sufferings,
particularly –
(make your request here)
–and that I may praise God with you
and all the saints forever.
I promise, O Blessed St. Jude,
to be ever mindful of this great favor
granted me by God
and to always honor you as my special
and powerful patron,
and to gratefully encourage devotion to you.
Amen

Chapter 6

Can You Find Her?

I was back in San Diego, in my office, when the phone rang. It was Frank calling from Special Care Hospital where he had recently been admitted.

"Hi, Dad, what's up?"

"Your mother was supposed to come to the hospital this morning. We had arranged to meet with Dr. D. here in my room. She is an hour late; can you find her?"

My mother is really smart and an excellent math teacher, but she has absolutely no sense of direction. She could get lost in Wilkes-Barre, the town where she was born and raised and had lived nearby for most of her life. But adding a lot of stress, a little confusion, and possibly dementia to the equation made a phone call reporting that she is lost seem inevitable.

After dad's recent bout of pneumonia, he needed rehab and Special Care Hospital looked like the best fit. It had both rehab and good medical care and—perhaps more importantly—his doctor, the local icon of geriatric care, was in residence there. Dr. D., the consummate small-town doc, complete with horned rimmed glasses and a quarter zip sweater, looked like he stepped right out of a Norman Rockwell painting. He was extremely compassionate and well-versed in caring for the aging, though he was aging too. Since Dr. D. is seventy-eight and my dad is eighty-two, you can't help but debate the pros and cons of having a physician that could be facing the same issues his patients were.

The only downside to Special Care Hospital was the difficult drive for mom to get there. After the usual winding road down the mountain, she had to merge several times on and off highways with trucks screaming by at sixty-five mph, then negotiate a difficult intersection where several deadly crashes had occurred. Mom, the proverbial little old lady who only drove to church and the grocery store, had been faithfully following Frank all summer as he was moved in and out of several hospitals and rehab facilities all over town. How she kept up with it we weren't sure, but she kept motoring along in a white twenty-year-old Mercury Sable that she refused to part with. Reluctant to make any changes in her life, she just kept clinging tighter and tighter to what she knew.

My sisters and I had argued about "taking the keys." There wasn't objective evidence for doing so; it was more a hunch that mom shouldn't be driving. Maybe she was a little more confused at this point; maybe her night vision wasn't good. It was an awkward conversation to have with anyone, let alone someone so headstrong. We knew mom wouldn't take it well. Just three months ago she had been furious, thinking it was premeditated when one of my sisters had mistakenly picked up her car keys. We finally agreed that Dr. D. could offer an objective evaluation or recommendation, so we nervously made the phone call asking him to make an assessment. But as far as we knew, nothing came of it. There was no follow up. Unfortunately, we didn't know that some states offer the option that someone like mom could be called in to take a driver's license re-test. The state simply summons the driver for a test without divulging that it was initiated by a family member or friend. The result is an objective evaluation of a driver's ability to be on the roads. If the driver fails, it is the state that "takes the keys." If only we had known.

I called my sisters to let them know that mom was missing. She hadn't shown up at Special Care Hospital for dad's appointment and wasn't answering the phone at home. Dad was very worried. Unfortunately, all three of us were far away. Mari lived near Mountain Top, in Scranton, Pennsylvania, but was on vacation in Florida and Ellyn was at her home in Sacramento, California. Mari offered to call the neighbors to check if mom's car was still in the garage. I called every police department between Mountain Top and Special Care Hospital. All I could do was leave a message on several answering machines until I got to Hanover Township. I got a real person, finally.

"Did you have any accidents in the area this morning?"

"There was a bad one on Sans Souci Highway."

My heart skipped a beat, but I quickly told myself that mom wouldn't have been on that road.

"Do you know what kind of cars were in the accident?"

"No."

With a really sick feeling in my stomach, I left my name and phone number. At my desk in San Diego, I searched the internet and found "Accident on Sans Souci Parkway, Hanover Township, PA." There on my desktop computer I saw the photo of a white Mercury Sable up on the median strip of the highway, a black truck adjacent to the driver's side. On the far side of the highway, the Dundee Garden Center provided a beautiful, peaceful fall backdrop of bright orange pumpkins, sunny yellow mums, and trees painted in fall foliage—all my mother's favorite things. Above the photo a caption in bold letters read: "WOMAN

DIES IN ACCIDENT." Clinging to hope, stuffing down what I didn't want to be true, yet already knowing, I waited for a phone call. I could keep up the pretense until the phone finally rang.

"This is Sheriff J., from Hanover Township. Are you the daughter of Joan Madden?"

"Yes."

"Joan has been killed in a car accident."

Oh God, help us.

"Joan's car was in a collision with another vehicle. It is not clear at this point what exactly transpired."

My mind started racing. I needed to call dad. I needed to call Mari and Ellyn. How do you put this terrible news into words? How do you console them? How can anyone be prepared for a thing like this?

The phone rang again. It was Mrs. Foley, who had gone down to the house to see if mom was still there. Instead she met several police officers trying to locate family members. Thank you, God, for Mrs. Foley. She told me she had called St. Jude's and Fr. Gerry was already on his way down to the hospital to break the news gently to Frank and to pray with him. Having gone through this before, she knew Frank should not be alone when he received this tragic news.

My old scuba diving mantra kicked in, "Stop, breathe, think." Deep breath, deep breath. Think. OK, just wait a few more minutes to give Fr. Gerry time to get there before calling dad. I better call Mari and Ellyn.

"Mom was in a terrible accident. . . . She didn't make it."

We were all in shock. The pain was too great. We could scarcely take it in. The phone rang again. It was dad.

"Did you find her?"

"Um, yeah. I found her."

"She was in an accident, wasn't she?"

"Yes, she was."

I prayed the fastest prayer for wisdom, fortitude, counsel, and piety. Come Holy Spirit, come right now! Obviously, Fr. Gerry wasn't there yet. I didn't want to tell my dad over the phone that mom had died that morning in a car accident on her way to see him. I didn't want any of this. But there is no outfoxing my dad. He could see through any story before you even started to tell it.

"What hospital did they take her to?"

"Mercy Hospital."

"Was it bad?"

"Yes, it was bad."

"Did she make it?"

"No, Dad, she didn't"

All I wanted was to be there with him right then and take away all his pain. I wanted to hug him and stay by his side. I wanted to be strong for him. But "Keep at it, Riley" was about to take on a whole new and deeper meaning. My strong "fighting Irish" dad was just about to begin the biggest fight of his life! He was about to "*be* strength" and "*teach* strength" to all of us!

I called my husband, Peter, and my children. Every time I had to repeat out loud what had happened, the words seemed to tear a deeper hole into my heart, and I couldn't bear to bring the pain upon those that will hear it. There was no way around it. Just be gentle.

"Grandma was in a car accident this morning. She didn't make it. The angels came and took her to heaven."

I began the long trek to Mountain Top, stopping at the airport bar to have a gin and tonic, my mother's favorite drink, to try to dull the agony. I was meeting Mari and her husband, Jim, at the Philadelphia airport to drive up to Mountain Top together.

When I laid eyes on Mari, I felt relief to be in the company of someone else who was going through the same pain I was. She gave me the update on what had happened while I was flying cross-country slumped in my own little stupor. Jim's sister, Mary, and her husband, David, went immediately to be with dad, and they stayed beside him until our first cousins, Pat and Greg could get there from South Jersey. When they heard the news about mom they dropped everything, leaving work and family to be with dad. God Bless them! Holy Spirit, you did answer me!

About two in the morning we finally pulled into the driveway in Mountain Top. The same driveway where we learned to drive, where we learned to roller skate, built snow forts, and had acorn fights. Walking up the steps to where mom had met us, welcoming us, countless times, where she would never be welcoming us again, made every step excruciating. But before we got to the top, Pat and Greg welcomed us with the biggest warmest hugs that just swept us up out of our grief and into loving arms, meeting us in our pain. As long as I live, I'll never be able to repay them for that moment. I was grateful I didn't have to walk into the dark house that my mother had left just hours ago full of hope and promise for the day, never to return. I only hope that I could be so kind as to drop everything to be there for Pat and Greg, or anyone else in such a moment of need.

I wasn't sure what state the house would be in. After all, mom had been running the household on her own, dashing off to the hospital every day to be with dad. I shouldn't have been surprised to find her bed made, not a dish in the sink, and every bill paid. Mom may have been under duress, but she was doing everything and doing it well.

Hail Mary

Hail Mary, full of grace
The Lord is with you
Blessed are you among women
and blessed is the fruit of your womb,
Jesus.

Holy Mary, Mother of God,
pray for us sinners,
now, and at the hour
of our death.
Amen.

Chapter 7

A Holy Death

Lying in my childhood bedroom, right next to my parents' empty bedroom, I woke up early in the autumn morning to the eerie sound of acorns rolling across the roof. Though I had managed only a couple of hours of sleep, I quietly rose, washed my tear-stained face and slipped out of the house to get to St. Jude's for the 7:00 a.m. Mass. I felt drawn to be where mom spent decades praying, talking with God, the saints, and all her friends. I wanted to be in her place of prayer, with her praying community.

I crept down the aisle of the church, slid into my mother's pew, and set my knees into her well-worn kneeler. All the heads turned and looked at me as if they were seeing a ghost. Aunt Mary, mom's cousin, slipped in next to me and held my hand. Our fingers intertwined, covered in freckled wrinkly skin identical to mom's. Mom had knelt here just yesterday morning on this same kneeler. She had received Holy Communion here just hours before she went home to God.

"LORD, hear my prayer; let my cry come to you. Do not hide your face from me in the day of my distress. Turn your ear to me; when I call, answer me quickly" (Ps 102:2-3). I prayed for mom. I prayed for dad. I prayed for my sisters and our families. I prayed for all those traveling. Oh please, no more accidents.

I prayed for Joe, the driver of the other vehicle. Lawyers and family had advised me not to contact Joe, but I knew my mother would have wanted him to be consoled. She would want him to know that she is in heaven now and so happy to be there. This life on earth is merely a preparation for our eternal reward with God. Mom would want Joe to move forward from this accident to become the best he could be, using all the gifts that God has given him. And most of all, she would pray that one day he would join her in heaven. All this was bursting in my heart to tell him, but how? I offered a fervent prayer to God to show me the way.

After Mass, like a funeral receiving line, everyone came forward to offer their condolences. The outpouring of love and sympathy from the St. Jude's morning Mass community surrounded me in a cloak of prayer that would see me through the next few days. The bond of the community that prays together, day after day, calls on the strong to lift up those that are weak. This morning, I was the weak earthen vessel that the strong filled to overflowing with divine love and prayer.

As if in a trance, I left St. Jude's and picked up my sister Mari at the house so we could go down to be with dad at the hospital. We had to make the same drive that we cautioned mom not to make because it was too dangerous. As we wound our way down the mountain road, the fall colors on the leaves welcomed us to our Pennsylvania home. We merged on and off Interstate 81, infamous for its speeding semi-trucks and fatal accidents. We negotiated the hairpin turn to access Route 29, and then, there it was, right in front of us. Sobs escaped uncontrollably as we arrived at the very spot where mom was taken up into heaven, where heaven and earth had met. It was on this holy ground that the angels came and lifted her home to God.

Only one mile later we arrived at Special Care Hospital. Mom had almost made it to the hospital. She was so close. What happened?

Mari and I walked in the front doors, passing our second cousin, Rona, in admissions, and continued up to the second floor. With a lump in my throat, I went quickly to dad and hugged the biggest, strongest man who had been made small and weak by this terrible blow.

"Dad, you know she's in heaven now."

"Well, if she's not, no one is going."

"I know. She never said a bad word about anyone."

"No. She never told a lie either, though it might have made things a lot easier at times."

We all laughed. As always, dad is the one in charge. He is the one comforting us.

"I've only been here for a week but everyone in the hospital had a nickname for your mother—Mrs. Hollywood. She always dressed to the nines in her high heels. She had a diamond on at least six fingers, and those *glasses*."

That got another laugh. We had all been on mom's case to update her "diamond" encrusted glasses. She liked them and that was that! Mrs. Hollywood was a perfect nickname. She did everything with style and class. And now we were determined to make sure her funeral celebrations were up to her standards.

I called St. Jude's to make the funeral arrangements. The associate, Fr. Gerry, answered.

"Fr. Gerry, thank you so much for going down to the hospital to be with dad yesterday."

"I was so glad to be there with him. But you know he is very strong."

"Fr. Gerry, I just went through mom's purse. It's not too surprising that she had a Sunday bulletin, and the last check she wrote was to St. Jude's."

"Oh yes, of course. I know she was at 11:15 a.m. Mass on Sunday because I was the celebrant. She came into the sacristy after Mass to offer me some suggestions on my homily."

"Oh, dear."

"No, no. They were good suggestions. I always welcomed a good conversation with your mom about theology."

"That's good, I enjoyed that too. It's one of the things I am going to miss terribly."

Ouch.

"Mom said to me more than once that she wanted to go to Mass on Sunday and be buried by Saturday."

"Well, it looks like we can make that happen. We can have her vigil on Friday night and her funeral liturgy on Saturday."

Carried by Angels

Escorted in such splendor
If you could only see
The beauty and the majesty
As angels carried me

Far beyond the life I knew
Secure in their embrace
My journey was a prelude
The glory of this place

Welcomed by rejoicing
No tears are ever found
God himself wipes them away
And angels' songs abound

Eternal gates were opened
Peace met me there inside
I rejoice now with the angels
In Heaven I abide

Sherrie Bradley Neal

Chapter 8

Keep Watch

Tim Finnegan's Wake

One morning Tim got rather full,
his head felt heavy which made him shake.
Fell from a ladder and he broke his skull,
and they carried him home his corpse to wake.
Rolled him up in a nice clean sheet,
and laid him out upon the bed
With a bottle of whiskey at his feet
and a barrel of porter at his head.

. . .

Mickey Maloney ducked his head
when a bottle of whiskey flew at him.
It missed, and falling on the bed,
the liquor scattered over Tim.
Now the spirits new life gave the corpse, my joy!
Tim jumped like a Trojan from the bed.
Cryin' will ye wallop each girl and boy,
t'underin' Jaysus, do ye think I'm dead?"

Having buried my grandparents, aunts, and uncles, I had experienced firsthand the many blessings a grieving family can receive from celebrating the progression of Catholic funeral rites. The root word for funeral, *funus*, implies procession. The Order of Christian Funerals ritualizes the procession starting with the Vigil of the Deceased at the funeral home, continuing to the Funeral Liturgy at the church, and lastly arriving at the cemetery for the Rite of Committal. Spanning several days, the procession of the body commemorates the completion of the Christian pilgrimage toward the heavenly kingdom begun at baptism, and invites family and mourners to accompany loved ones on their final passage and commend them to God.

I knew I could count on my family to set aside time from their everyday life to come together to pray and mourn the passing of mom. Since news travels fast in my family, I was certain that within hours after the date for mom's funeral Mass was set, cousins all across the country would have their bags packed and be on their way to Mountain Top.

The Vigil would be the first opportunity for many of our family and friends to be together after receiving the news of mom's death. We could gather in the presence of her body to pray for her and all those who mourned her loss. It would give us a chance to connect and share our grief and our stories before the funeral Mass the next day.

To keep vigil means to keep watch, to wait and pray during a time usually meant for sleeping, in anticipation for something to happen. The Irish Vigil is known as "The Wake," which means to stay awake and watch over the body through the night until they are buried the next day. Some suggest that an attentive eye over the corpse was needed in case they weren't really dead after all. And that was certainly true in the case of Tim Finnegan. According to his famed ballad, Tim awoke in the middle of his very own wake!

In Mom Conway's day, she and other women would come into the home of the deceased to wash the body and prepare it to be "laid-out" in the front room of the house they called the "parlor." That's why we still hear funeral homes referred to as "funeral parlors." Mom Conway would also have given your parlor an upgrade by borrowing better rugs, paintings, and furniture from around the neighborhood. Today she'd be called a home stager, making sure you were looking good for the party. Party?

Well, absolutely. It's the Irish custom to honor their dead and to pay their respects to the family by showing up at the house with their arms full of food and whiskey. It is probably no coincidence that the Irish name for whiskey is *Uisce beatha*, water of life. Irish monks in the Middle Ages had astutely recognized the benefits of distilled spirits and gave them their fitting name. Whiskey at the wake is not so much to drown your sorrows but to toast a life well lived while sharing memories, both funny and sad. And whiskey certainly animates the celebration.

Irish wake traditions include hints of superstition, like covering the mirrors and opening the windows so the spirit of the deceased can exit the house and make its way to heaven yet hiding their boots so they can't walk off. Clocks were stopped at the time of death to confuse the devil. As the Irish toast reveals: "May your glass be ever full. May the roof over your head be always strong. And may you be in heaven half an hour before the devil knows you're dead." And just to be sure, the windows were closed the next morning to keep the devil from coming in.

Trays of white clay pipes, tobacco, and snuff were an important part of the wake. The snuff was inhaled into both nostrils as a rite of purification. The shank of the clay pipe could be dipped into Guinness or whiskey to add flavor. When you received one it was customary to say, "Lord have mercy" so the pipe came to be called a "Lord ha' mercy."

On the morning of the funeral, the body was carried out onto the porch in the open casket and placed upon four chairs, one for each of the evangelists, Matthew, Mark, Luke, and John. The women arrived wearing a black mantilla and the men wore a triangular piece of black cloth pinned on their left shoulder, symbolizing that their loved one is now resting with the Holy Trinity. Just before the coffin was closed, mourners would kiss their deceased loved one and pay their last respects. Then the pallbearers gently lifted the coffin unto to their shoulders and reverently carried it in procession to the church.

The wake for my grandfather, Jack Madden, was certainly one of the most memorable. Aunts, uncles, first and second cousins filled the house with love and laughter, retelling the stories of the treasured man that he was. Somehow the joy that Jack brought to everyone throughout his life was rekindled and relived at the wake.

Some of our favorite stories came from our annual Easter trips to visit Frank's sister, Aunt Joan Marie. She was a pioneer. Never married, she started her career in the 1950s working at the Pentagon as a computer programmer for the Air Force. Every spring Jack, Anna, mom, dad, Mari, Ellyn, and I would pour ourselves into a Chevy Bel Air and make the six hour drive from Mountain Top down to Washington, DC. We would enjoy playing tourist, visiting the Smithsonian Institute, the cherry blossoms around the Tidal Basin, and celebrate Easter Sunday at St. Matthew's Cathedral. But on one particular trip we decided to tour the United States Capitol building.

Now, Jack always turned heads. He moved with an easy stride, invariably stretched to his full height of 6' 2" with shoulders back and perfect posture. A full head of white hair, brushed straight back, crowned his striking, distinguished look. So, it wasn't too surprising that as we toured the Capitol, a complete stranger approached Jack and said:

"Excuse me, Senator, can you tell me how to get to the Russell Senate Office Building?"

We laughed until it hurt, and forever more, blurting out the occasional, "Excuse me, Senator" guaranteed another episode of the giggles.

That night we stayed at Aunt Joan Marie's apartment and after a few rounds of the Jameson fell sound asleep.

The next morning, we laughed even harder. Maybe it was waking up in an unfamiliar house, or maybe it was the Irish whiskey, but in the middle of the night Jack had mistaken the coat closet for a water closet. Excuse me, Senator!

Death is Nothing at All

Death is nothing at all
I have only slipped away to the next room.
I am I and you are you.
Whatever we were to each other,
That, we still are.

Call me by my old familiar name.
Speak to me in the easy way
which you always used.
Put no difference into your tone.
Wear no forced air of solemnity or sorrow.

Laugh as we always laughed
at the little jokes we enjoyed together.
Play, smile, think of me. Pray for me.
Let my name be ever the household word
that it always was.
Let it be spoken without effect.
Without the trace of a shadow on it.

Life means all that it ever meant.
It is the same that it ever was.
There is absolute unbroken continuity.
Why should I be out of mind
because I am out of sight?

I am but waiting for you.
For an interval.
Somewhere. Very near.
Just around the corner.

All is well.
Nothing is past; nothing is lost.
One brief moment and all will be as it was before only better,
infinitely happier and forever we will all be one together with Christ.

Henry Scott Holland
(as adapted by the Carmelite monks in Tallow, County Waterford)

Chapter 9

The Bride of Christ

I met with George, director of the Mountain Top Funeral Home, to arrange for mom's Vigil. It felt all wrong. Mom was always the one that took care of the family's funeral arrangements. It was beginning to hit home that she was gone. But George thoughtfully walked me through all the decisions that had to be made—picking out the casket, the schedule, the flowers, and the prayer cards.

I expected that George would be competent in his work at the funeral parlor, but it was a welcome surprise that he was also a very kind and compassionate man. He obviously learned in mortician school how to prepare the body and make all the arrangements, but genuine sympathy and patience for grieving families can't be taught; it is a gift. He had a calmness about him that put me at ease as much as was humanly possible. It was obvious that for George this wasn't just a job; he has answered God's call to minister to the bereaved. What came next was easier to accept because of George's demeanor.

"We may need to have a closed casket. The accident was bad. She had some injuries to her head."

What, no open casket? In the last few years my mother had spent much of her free time going to wakes and funerals. Every wake was sure to be followed with the "Wake Report." Mom would call to let me know that the deceased looked "so good." And then came the canonization. It was as if death erased all their faults and failings and the pope himself had declared the deceased a saint. It was just like the traditional Irish keening that chanted praises for the dead with a litany of all the good works they had done throughout their lifetime. My Nana was a keener, one of the Irish women that offered the ritual Gaelic wailing after the corpse was "laid-out." Keeners were often paid to come and outwardly display emotions the family bottled up inside, maintaining a stoic face in public. The keener's sung lament encircled the corpse and the bereaved, holding them close, and softening their departure. Since the church discouraged it as a pagan practice meant to ward off evil spirits, it has fallen out of custom. But I'd like to think of keening as the gift of seeing the deceased with the merciful eyes of God instead of the judgmental eyes of a human sinner.

My mother, the modern-day keener, provided a running commentary after every wake on how good the deceased looked, what a wonderful person they were, and all the people that came to pay their respects. The way she described the deceased you could almost forget the person was dead. Yet, in faith we know it is only their time on earth that has come to an end. They have been called home to God. The angels came to take them up to heaven.

So, of course it was important to mom and to all the family that she too looked "so good." After I processed the closed casket part, it finally sunk in that mom had severe head injuries. I couldn't think about that. I could only pray that her death was instantaneous. Please God, I hope she did not suffer.

Whether the casket would be open or closed, I still had to choose an outfit for Mrs. Hollywood. Knowing that I was the black sheep of the family when it came to clothes didn't help. It was common knowledge that I would rather stick needles in my eyes than go shopping, but the rest of the women in the family were all shoppers. Got a spare couple of hours? Go shopping!

Modern technology was going to see me through this. I went through mom's many closets, pulling outfits out, taking pictures with my phone and sending them to my sisters. The three of us quickly agreed on an elegant silver suit. Ok, outfit picked! Next came the accessorizing. Mom never went without the correct jewelry, scarf, purse, and shoes. She always made it look so easy, having everything coordinated to perfection. We could not let her down. Fortunately, we easily agreed on a triple-strand pearl necklace. It was obvious that the grace of God was getting us through this.

But then it came to the undergarments. I felt like I had hit a stone wall. I searched through her drawers and found nothing that seemed worthy. It was all too symbolic that everything visible was neat and tidy and in control, but underneath, things had been unraveling, literally.

All of a sudden it came over me. She was going home to God. As a member of the Church, she was a bride of Christ. "As a young man marries a virgin, your Builder shall marry you; and as a bridegroom rejoices in his bride so shall your God rejoice in you" (Is 62:5). She was going to the wedding feast. She needed to be dressed appropriately.

> The servants went out into the streets
> and gathered all they found,
> bad and good alike, and the hall was filled with guests.
> But when the king came in to meet the guests
> he saw a man there not dressed in a wedding garment.
> He said to him,
> "My friend, how is it that you came in here
> without a wedding garment?"
> But he was reduced to silence.
>
> (Mt 22:8-12)

I would have to buy something. I may have avoided the mall in the past, but I could go now; I could go for my mom. I headed bravely to Victoria's Secret. Arriving at the store without really thinking this through, I was blindsided when the clerk asked me,

"Can I help you?"

I did not know how to answer. Do I tell her it is for a corpse? Ok, that's a definite no!

"What size are you looking for? Would you like to be measured?"

Sweet Jesus, what do I say?

"Oh, no—uh, it's not for me. It's a—it's a gift." I make up a size. . ."I am looking for something in white maybe with a little lace."

She gave me several choices, several patterns, several sizes. Too many choices. I was suddenly overwhelmed. It was definitely a combination of paralyzing grief and the shopping issue. In days and weeks and months to come I would recognize these moments of grief paralysis. Something triggered a memory or an emotion, and I'd be struck with grief—stopped in my tracks and finding it difficult to go on.

I stood, stalled. I breathed in slowly, then whispered my fervent prayer, "I arise today through God's strength to pilot me; God's might to uphold me, God's wisdom to guide me, God's eye to look before me, God's ear to hear me, God's word to speak for me, God's hand to guard me, God's way to lie before me, God's shield to protect me. . . . Amen."

The moment passed. I collected myself enough to pick out a beautiful white lace set and a bridal slip. Mom would now be appropriately dressed as a bride of Christ. While scripture comments on the need for the appropriate outer garments for the wedding feast, it is really what is in our heart that must be right with God. Certainly, mom had that covered. "Well done my good and faithful servant" (Mt. 25:21). In honoring her as God's creation, made in the image and likeness of God, and an adopted child of God in baptism, her body was to be treated with all the dignity she deserved.

On Thursday afternoon, as I dropped off mom's clothes at the funeral home, George came out to talk with me.

"It looks like we will be able to have an opened casket after all."

The bells rang, the angels sang, and the gates of heaven opened!

"Thanks be to God! What a relief."

"It is part of our protocol to invite the immediate family in for a pre-viewing before the wake. Would you and your sisters be able to come over tomorrow at about 2:00 p.m.?"

"Yes, thank you. I can arrange that."

"Ok. Very good. The flowers are all ordered. The parlor will be filled with daisies, your mom's favorite flowers. Would you like to see the prayer cards? They were just delivered."

Choosing a prayer card for a deceased loved one is a special honor. On the front is the image of a saint that they may have had a special devotion to and on the back is a cherished prayer. Since my mother was devoted to all the saints, how could we go wrong? But we chose the Madonna of the Streets, the image that was hanging in her bedroom for as long as we could remember. The prayer on the back was the poem "Carried by Angels," by Sherrie Bradley Neal. It so perfectly described how the angels had come to carry mom home to heaven.

I turned back to George and said, "Thank you so much, for taking good care of us. We sincerely appreciate it. We will see you tomorrow."

The next day Mari, Ellyn, and I walked into the funeral parlor, fearful and with heavy hearts. George, kind and considerate as always, gently led us into the room where mom was. We were greeted by dozens and dozens of daisies, which made us smile. Ever so gingerly, we walked toward the casket and gathered around mom, tears rolling down our cheeks. As we said a quiet prayer for her, we couldn't help but wonder what she had gone through in the accident. Yet we were consoled knowing that St. Peter would surely let her in the pearly gates.

She was so still, so quiet, like she was just sleeping. But when I reached out and touched her hand as if to wake her, I felt the icy coldness. The reality of her death began to sink into my bones. She is not here. She is in heaven and certainly deserves her heavenly reward. And thankfully, she did look "so good," smartly dressed and accessorized as always. It was such a relief to know that she would have the wake that she wanted.

Then, Ellyn quietly whispered, "Should I take a picture to show dad? It might prepare him for seeing her in person."

Since Ellyn was going down to Special Care Hospital to bring Frank up to the wake, she would have the opportunity to do that. I quickly replied, "Ellyn, I think that's a good idea. It will be hard on him to arrive here unprepared for what he will find."

Mari wholeheartedly agreed.

We planned to meet back at the funeral home at 6:30 before the doors opened at 7:00 for the public. As we said good-bye, we hugged and felt grateful that we had each other to lean on during this tragic time.

I returned to my parents' house to get dressed for the wake and found myself amid a commotion that resembled a cross between a deli, a bakery, and a liquor store. Food and alcohol had been flowing into the house nonstop. It was like the loaves and the fishes. Friends and neighbors were lined up with cases of water, beer, toilet paper, tissues, bagels, and more. Their sympathy and compassion poured out in the form of food and drink to soothe our pain and sorrow.

It started to dawn on me that people would be coming over to the house after the Vigil. We would need to organize food, plates, and napkins. I was starting to feel overwhelmed again. The phone rang. My cousin Sue was on the line.

"It's Sue, what can we do?"

Sue's husband Paul, a successful engineer, has a hobby—cooking! He'll know what to do with all this food.

"Sue, we have lots of food here that needs to be put out after the wake. Can you and Paul help sort this out?"

Sue, without hesitation, said reassuringly, "We are coming over. Don't worry."

Then Mari chimed in, "Mary and David are coming over to help out at the house!"

Relieved, I said, "That's just what we need! Praise God!"

Meanwhile, Ellyn and her husband Andy had gone down to Special Care Hospital to get Frank ready for the wake. After they arrived, Dr. D. took Ellyn aside to give some last-minute instructions, along with a few medications. The doctor warned that tonight and tomorrow would be very stressful on Frank and could easily trigger a heart attack. By now, Ellyn thought she could use some medications herself, but of the alcoholic kind, like maybe a birdbath of Bailey's Irish Cream.

It was harder to get Frank dressed than anticipated. After receiving the news of mom's death, his physical strength had weakened by the moment. And now, today he could no longer stand. Ellyn and Andy had to use all their wisdom and strength to get Frank's suit on him. After he was all set, Ellyn thought that this would be the time to show him the picture of mom. Reluctantly, she said, "Dad, I have a picture of mom in the casket."

"OK."

Ellyn pulled up the photo on her phone and hesitantly showed it to Frank. The color drained from his face. Stunned, he drew in a deep breath. Then, as if the reality of it hit him for the first time, he stammered, "She's dead." Tears rolled down their cheeks. Ellyn hugged dad.

5

Arise and Come

My lover speaks and says to me,
"Arise, my friend, my beautiful one, and come!
For see, the winter is past,
the rains are over and gone.
The flowers appear on the earth,
the time of pruning the vines has come,
and the song of the turtledove is heard in our land.
The fig tree puts forth its figs,
and the vines, in bloom, give forth fragrance.
Arise, my friend, my beautiful one, and come!"

(Sg 2:10-13)

Chapter 10

Joan R. Madden's Wake

Before anyone else arrived at the funeral home, Peter—my husband and my rock—and our three children, Greg, Kelley, and Mollie, walked into the parlor where mom was laid out. We inched our way to the casket and gathered around her so our children could pray for their grandma. They were very close to her, and the news of her sudden death had come as a terrible shock. This was the first death my children had experienced, and I was grateful that I could accompany them through the treasured Funeral Rites of the Catholic Church, rites celebrated by my ancestors for countless generations that witnessed our deep faith. I hoped and prayed that our children would celebrate them for me and Peter when the angels come for us.

My heart sank as I watched my father enter the room. Andy slowly pushed him in his wheelchair towards the casket. Ellyn had prepared me that dad had weakened significantly and after seeing the picture of mom in the casket had remained understandably sullen and quiet. My eyes followed him closely as he drew next to mom. His head nodded in prayer, seemingly in recognition that God had called her home. He tenderly patted the hand that bore the diamond ring he had given her sixty years earlier. Without a tear in his eye, he held his chin firm, and squared his broad shoulders. Right before us, he seemed to strengthen. Only God could be miraculously holding him up right now.

We set up the receiving line. Dad, in his wheelchair, was right next to the casket. Mari, being the oldest, was after dad, then me, then Ellyn and our spouses next to each of us for support. People started coming in . . . neighbors, friends, relatives, priests, nuns, students, and students' parents. When Aunt Nancy, mom's only sibling walked in, it was a good thing Uncle Johnny had one arm and Pat had the other. After seeing mom in the casket, Nancy's legs buckled right out from under her.

As people streamed in, they stopped to kneel before mom and say a prayer. Then they slowly made their way through the line offering their words of condolence. Frank continued to demonstrate his renewed God-given strength by welcoming our guests as the patriarch of the family, thanking one and all for coming. Until I was on the receiving end, I couldn't know what a comfort it was to see familiar faces of loved ones gathering and offering their prayers and support. Their presence alone provided deep consolation.

Then it suddenly got quiet. Mari whispered, "It's him. He's here. The other driver in the accident."

She pointed to the young man kneeling, praying, at mom's side. Then slowly, he rose and turned. I went straight up to him. The words started pouring out of my mouth, as if scripted by a divine voice,

"My mother is in heaven now. She is in a better place. She is very happy. She would not want this to bother you. She would want you to go on to do good things with your life. Be the best that you can be. You are not to let this bring you down, for she is surely in heaven now."

I noticed the woman alongside him, tears streaming down her cheeks, mouthing, "Thank you, thank you."

Through her sobs the woman stammered, "I am his mother, but it was his idea to come here. You see, I was one of your mother's students."

The anguish this poor mother was enduring was painfully visible. They came to console us, but instead, I wanted to console and comfort this suffering mother and son. As warmly as I could, I said, "My mother is in heaven now. The angels came and took her straight up to heaven," I added tenderly, "Thank you so much for being here. I'm so glad you came tonight."

It was the answer to my fervent prayer. I had hoped against hope for this opportunity to reach out to him. Frank, however, didn't have the same reaction. Though I know it was just his protective instincts speaking, Frank said he just wanted to deck him. It was the only time I was ever grateful that dad was confined to the wheelchair.

Deacon Kovach, from St. Jude's, arrived to lead the prayers for the Vigil for the Deceased. It was perfect timing to turn our hearts and minds to God in praise for the wonderful creation of mom, to pray for her reception into the heavenly banquet, and for the comfort of all the gathered who mourn. We particularly lifted up Frank who was left without his life partner and advocate. And in the silence of my heart, I lifted up the driver of the other vehicle.

We had only scheduled two hours at the funeral home for visitors but now we were getting close to three. People kept streaming in, friends from our childhood, from our neighborhood, and from St. Jude's parish. We lost count of the number of priests that came. Though there were many familiar faces, there were even more that we had never met before. All the stories of mom's students over the years seemed to take flesh as one after another arrived to offer their sympathy and introduce themselves.

I suddenly noticed that all the young people, the many cousins and second cousins, were missing from the room. I motioned for Ellen Schmidt, my friend since we were babies, to come over.

"Ellen, where did all the kids go?"

"Uh, Noreen. They are all out in the parking lot."

"The parking lot? What are they doing out in the parking lot?"

"I went outside looking for them and saw them hanging around the trunk of a car. As I got closer, I noticed they all had their hands behind their backs. So, I asked, 'All right, what are you up to?' They said they were just taking a break. I told them I wasn't born yesterday. Then, from behind their backs, one by one, out came the beers. So, maybe it wasn't my best response, but I asked, 'Do you have one more for me?'"

"Nice one, Ellen."

"Then Uncle Jack started walking toward us, so we all hid the beers behind our backs. But you can't fool Uncle Jack. He figured it out right away and started scolding us for drinking at the wake. And as soon as he was finished yelling at us, he asked, 'Well, aren't you going to offer me one?'"

I laughed and said, "Got to love Uncle Jack."

After the wake many went back to the house for food, conversation, and libations, not necessarily in that order. As if we did not have enough weight upon us with my mother's sudden and tragic death, Frank couldn't join the gathering in the kitchen. He got out of the car and into the garage but couldn't make it up the steps into the house. The news of mom's death had taken away whatever remaining strength he had in his legs. For just a short while, Frank stoically stayed down in the garage with a few of his close friends. Then Ellyn, with all her nursing skills, got him back into his van and drove him down to Special

Care Hospital where he needed to remain in rehab. Frank had been discharged only temporarily to attend the wake and the funeral the next day but was expected to remain as a resident patient. Ellyn, very lovingly, stayed overnight in the hospital with Frank. She did not want him alone this night. She wanted to be with him as he awoke in the morning to help him through this difficult time, to dress and accompany him to his wife's funeral Mass and burial. Yet, in this painful moment of loss and profound grief, what sustained Frank was knowing that mom was truly in a better place.

The Lord Will Wipe away Our Tears

On this mountain the LORD of hosts
will provide for all peoples
a feast of rich food and choice wines,
juicy, rich food and pure, choice wines.
On this mountain he will destroy the veil that veils all peoples,
the web that is woven over all nations.
He will destroy death forever.
The Lord GOD will wipe away the tears from all faces;
the reproach of his people he will remove from the whole earth;
for the LORD has spoken.
On that day it will be said:
"Indeed, this is our God; we looked to him, and he saved us!
This is the LORD to whom we looked;
let us rejoice and be glad that he has saved us!"

(Is 25:6-9)

73

Chapter 11

The Funeral Mass
for Joan R. Madden

The Madden family caravan, following the hearse, slowly processed through Mountain Top from the funeral home to St. Jude's Church for the funeral Mass for Joan R. Madden. Our aching hearts longed to gather with our community for Mass as we had for so many years. We yearned for the comfort of familiar faces in a familiar church praying familiar prayers. Celebrating the funeral Mass, we would have the opportunity to worship God together and to give thanks for the wondrous creation of Joan R. Madden.

Learning that Frank was now confined to a wheelchair, Fr. Joe, the pastor of St. Jude's, thoughtfully suggested that Frank slip into the church from the side door and wait at the front for Mass to begin. Having known Frank and Joan very well for many years, Fr. Joe sensed that coming down the center aisle in a wheelchair would only add to Frank's physical and mental anguish. But with amazing tenacity, Frank insisted upon entering the front door with Joan and his family. Frank was determined to accompany his bride as they processed down the aisle together towards the altar one last time.

The Funeral Rite began with family surrounding the casket at the threshold of the church for the Reception of the Body. Fr. Joe sprinkled mom's casket with holy water as a reminder of her baptism, when she was buried with Christ and rose to new life in him. Then the three daughters and five granddaughters gently draped a white pall over mom's casket, symbolizing the baptismal garment she had received when she became a Christian and had put on Christ. Just as baptism led us to the Eucharistic table, we processed down the center aisle towards the altar beginning with servers carrying the crucifix and candles, followed by Fr. Joe. The casket came next, guided by mom's grandson: Greg, sons-in-law: Peter, Jim, and Andy, and nephews: Greg, and Dave. Close behind came Frank in his wheelchair, pushed by nephew Pat. The Madden women— daughters: Mari, Noreen, and Ellyn, and granddaughters: Aileen, Kelley, Mollie, Haley, and Riley—followed Frank arm in arm.

As we made our way down the aisle, we were comforted to see the church filled to capacity with family, friends, and many of mom's students. But approaching the altar, we were surprised to see the president and six other Holy Cross priests from King's College in the sanctuary. Frank was a proud graduate of King's College and an active alumnus. He and Joan had enjoyed cheering on the basketball team at all their home games. But most of all, Frank relished being the top fundraiser each year as he skillfully teased out donations from his fellow alumni during the annual phone-a-thon. The presence of King's priests was a powerful testimony to their love and support for Joan but even more so for Frank. It was difficult enough for us to process the tragic news of mom's sudden death, but it was inconceivable that Frank, who had been at death's door so many times, was now burying his wife and lifeline. No one expected Frank to outlive mom and now we couldn't fathom how he would survive without her.

We needed to turn our hearts and minds to God and surrender to him all our anxieties and fears.

The Liturgy of the Word soothed us with familiar scriptures. The Gospel reading was the well-known passage describing the tension between the two sisters Martha and Mary (Lk 10:38-42). Martha complained to Jesus that Mary, merely sitting at Jesus's feet listening to him, left Martha to do all the work.

After the Gospel was proclaimed, Fr. Joe left the sanctuary and came down towards the assembly. Much to everyone's surprise he pulled out a large slate blackboard on wheels from the side chapel. He explained that Joan was obviously Martha. She worked very hard, year after year, as an excellent mathematics teacher at Crestwood High School. Crestwood's custodian, John, shared with him that Joan worked so hard that she would even wear out her blackboard. In fact, she needed a new blackboard every year. And interestingly, not one other teacher ever needed a new one.

But, Fr. Joe continued, Joan was also Mary. She found her strength right here in this church on her worn-out kneeler listening to Jesus. The Eucharistic Liturgy was truly the source and summit of her faith. Joan left Mass with the grace to go out to do the work of the Lord in the community. Suddenly, Fr. Joe flipped over the blackboard and on the other side we could read in large block letters: MISTAKES. He deftly pulled out an eraser and in seconds completely wiped away the word. He remarked, "Joan was a compassionate teacher who was known to offer a clean slate to every student that needed one. She was able to combine the gifts of Mary and Martha to serve her students with love and mercy. You see, Joan was Mary and Martha."

As Fr. Joe pushed the blackboard back into the side chapel and walked back up into the sanctuary, I said a quick prayer of gratitude for Fr. Joe and his consoling words. I prayed that Frank would be strengthened in faith and hope at this very moment.

As we celebrated the Liturgy of the Eucharist, the memorial of the Paschal mystery, our faith in the resurrection of the dead was renewed and strengthened at a time when we needed it most. Receiving the Blessed Sacrament, we were nourished with the Real Presence of Christ and brought into communion with one another, a unity we treasured and relied upon. We all knew that this celebration of the Holy Mass was just the foretaste of the heavenly banquet, where we hoped to one day join mom and all those that have gone before us in faith, in the presence of our Lord.

I had been invited to say a few words of remembrance after Communion. I prayed and practiced to ensure that I could convey the remarkable life of faith mom had led. For better or for worse, this is what I was inspired to say.

It is very curious that in Irish there isn't a word for "yes" or "no." Whatever that says about the Irish culture, it may explain why mom could never answer a question with a definitive "yes" or "no." Instead, much like Jesus, she would answer a question with a parable. Whether that meant that mom was a lot like Jesus or Jesus was Irish, I can't be sure. But nonetheless, I thought it would be quite fitting to use a parable to describe my mother today. So, I would like to recount the parable of the Murphy twins, Matt and Finn.

The Murphys were a lovely Irish family. There was the Mr. and the Mrs. and their handsome young twins, Matt and Finn. Though Mr. and Mrs. Murphy felt so blessed to have their fine young lads, they were a bit concerned about them. You see, Finn could find no bad in the world and Matt could find no good. With the one always smiling and the other always crying, they thought they better check in with Dr. O'Sullivan before this went on any longer.

"Dr. O'Sullivan, what should we do?"

"Oh, not to worry Mr. and Mrs. Murphy, I'll have them as right as rain in no time at all!"

"For Matt, you take a room and fill it with all the best toys in the land. Get the ones with all the bright lights, bells, and whistles, and anything else a boy his age would ever want. As for Finn, set up a room filled with nothing but horse manure. Put Matt in his room and Finn in his; lock the doors; wait ten minutes and then they'll be good to go!"

Now, Mr. and Mrs. Murphy were a little fearful about putting their lads through such a thing, but they loved them and wanted the best for them. So, they got to work; set up the two rooms; and sent in the lads.

They waited a long ten minutes till they could barely take any more of it.

Mrs. Murphy opened the door to Matt. He was in there crying his little eyes out.

"Oh, Matt. Come here, me boy. What are you crying about?"

"Mam, there's nothing good in here at all. This toy is broken. This one is too loud and this one is too bright."

"Oh, come here then Matt. It's all right. Not to worry dear."

Mr. Murphy gasped, "Dear Lord, we better go see how our Finn is doing."

As they approached the door to where Finn was, they heard whooping and hollering!

They slowly opened the door, fearful of what they'd find. There was Finn, throwing up fistfuls of manure into the air, and shouting with glee.

"Finn, dear, what <u>are</u> you doing?"

"Oh mam, with all this *shit* in here there must be a pony somewhere!"

I said *shit*! I had been practicing for two days, telling the parable over and over to any willing listener but I said the word "manure." I *never* said "shit." But each time I told the parable, it evoked vociferous complaints that I shouldn't say manure.

"Why do you say manure? We all know it's *shit*. Just say *shit*."

"We'll be in church. I am not saying *shit* in church and that's that."

But there it was. I just said "shit." If mom hadn't already died, she would die now for sure. And if she had been buried now, she'd certainly have rolled over in her grave. Is it too late to grab Fr. Joe's eraser and give myself a clean slate? There was nothing to do about it. I couldn't take the word back. I had to keep going.

You see, mom was just like Finn. She found the good in every situation and in every person. Through her eyes of faith, she could see every human being as a creation of God with a unique set of gifts and talents. Her gift was to look within each person and identify what their gifts and talents were. But she didn't leave it at that, she would zero in on them and draw them out of you. She persistently reminded you of your great potential and encouraged you to use your gifts to be the best that you could be.

For mom, it was part of her lifelong guiding principle as a Christian to live her life for others. Mom followed a tenet of Fr. Hesburgh, the revered Holy Cross priest, and President of the University of Notre Dame, that all of our Holy Cross priests here today are certainly familiar with. "Do as much as you can, for as many as you can, for as long as you can!" Mom served her family as a daughter, wife, mother, grandmother, sister, and aunt. She served the community as a high school math teacher and in her retirement was a member of the Mountain Top Zoning Board. She served her Church faithfully every Monday morning counting money and every summer working at the Church picnic plush animal booth.

I can personally testify that more than once in mom's life she found herself in a room full of manure but through the lens of faith, hope, and love of the Lord, she found that pony.

Let's follow mom's example and place our complete faith and trust in God. As St. Julian of Norwich put it, "All shall be well, and all shall be well, and all manner of thing shall be well."

Trust in the Lord

Blessed are those who trust in the LORD;
the LORD will be their trust.
They are like a tree planted beside the waters
that stretches out its roots to the stream:
It does not fear heat when it comes,
its leaves stay green;
In the year of drought it shows no distress,
but still produces fruit.

(Jer 17:7-8)

Chapter 12

Passing It On

The Wild Rover

I've been a wild rover for many's the year
And I've spent all me money on whiskey and beer
But now I'm returning with gold in great store
And I never will play the wild rover no more

And it's no, nay, never
No, nay never no more
Will I play the wild rover
No never no more

I'll go home to my parents, confess what I've done
And I'll ask them to pardon their prodigal son
And if they caress me, as oft times before
I never will play the wild rover no more

L eaving the funeral Mass for my mother, with deep gratitude for the uplifting prayers, we processed out the center aisle of the church to continue on to the cemetery for the Rite of Committal. As I made my way out the front door of St. Jude's, the same door my mother had carried me through to be baptized, I crossed a threshold into a new phase, a new time. Life would never be the same. As I tried to pull myself up straighter and stronger, a man approached me and abruptly said, "I was a student of your mother's. Which of her grandchildren is the best in math?"

"I'm, I'm not sure," I stuttered. I had trouble processing what he was saying, and I was reluctant to choose one grandchild over the others. I could hear my mother saying, they are all excellent at math! Mom even made sure her daughters married a man that could do math just to be sure the right genes were passed on to the next generation.

"I drove down from Binghamton, New York, to be here this morning."

"Oh, my goodness, that's two hours away, how kind of you to come!"

"You see, my brother and I were bad in high school. I mean really bad. My brother's still in jail. But there was something in me that your mother saw. I still don't know what or why, but she kept encouraging me to be the best that I could be. I kept at it and ended up going on to get my PhD in mathematics. I was so grateful for your mother's inspiration that I dedicated my thesis to her. I brought a copy of it with me today to give to her grandchild who is the best in math."

Still bewildered, I replied, "I'm not sure who is the best; they are all good at math."

I slowly opened his dissertation, and sure enough, there it was: "I dedicate this dissertation to Joan R. Madden. . ." and below it I instantly recognized my mother's signature.

"Well, when you figure it out, please give it to one of her grandchildren."

"This is so kind of you. Thank you for sharing your story. I will pass it on."

I gripped the thesis tightly like I was clinging onto mom's hand. Her tremendous gift was being passed on, reaching across time. The blessing that my mother bestowed upon this young man in the past was made present today to be forwarded to one of her grandchildren.

I was reminded that the Eucharist re-presents, makes present, the sacrifice of the cross on Calvary. The Eucharist is the sacrifice of the Body and Blood of Jesus that he instituted at the Last Supper to perpetuate the sacrifice of the cross through time, until he comes again. In receiving the Body of Christ, we are sent to bring Christ to the world. Christ asks us to "Do this in memory of me." We are asked to surrender our will for the will of the Father, to give up our lives for others, as Christ did.

This was a profound moment in my life, one in which I could feel the divine hand of God. Time can be measured in two ways, in *chronos* or *kairos*. *Chronos* time is measured in minutes, by the ticking of a clock. But *kairos* time is measured in moments, by noticing the indwelling of God in our lives, where time seems to stand still, to take in the depth and breadth of God. Without a doubt, this was a *kairos* moment.

I tucked the leather-bound thesis into my guitar case for a time when I could give it the attention it was due.

Amazing Grace

Amazing grace!
How sweet the sound
That saved a wretch like me!
I once was lost, but now I'm found;
Was blind, but now I see.

'Twas grace that taught my heart to fear,
And grace my fears relieved;
How precious did that grace appear
The hour I first believed.

The Lord has promised good to me,
His Word my hope secures;
He will my Shield and Portion be.
As long as life endures.

John Newton

Chapter 13

St. Mary's Cemetery

Dear Old Donegal

And now that I'm going back again
to dear old Erin's isle,
My friends will meet me on the pier
and greet me with a smile.
Their faces, sure, I've almost forgot,
I've been so long away,
But me mother will introduce them all
and this to me will say:

Meet Branigan, Fannigan, Milligan, Gilligan,
Duffy, McCuffy, Malachy, Mahone,
Rafferty, Lafferty, Donnelly, Connelly,
Dooley, O'Hooley, Muldowney, Malone,
Madigan, Cadigan, Lanihan, Flanihan, Fagan,
O'Hagan, O'Hoolihan, Flynn,
Shanihan, Manihan, Fogarty, Hogarty, Kelly,
O'Kelly, McGuinness, McGuinn.

Steve Graham

A stroll through St. Mary's Cemetery made you think
you had stumbled upon the directory for the Irish
section in heaven. It was the unliving proof of the
Irish diaspora. Reading the names on the tombstones was
like singing a verse of "Dear Old Donegal": Conway, Coyle,
Costigan, Gorman, Manion, Madden, Miller, McCarty,
Whelley, Wall, Foley, Feeney, Finnerty, Haley, Henry, and
Judge. Mom would be buried alongside her beloved parents,

in-laws, and many relatives and friends in a lush green hill-side, under a canopy of trees in northeastern Pennsylvania that could easily be mistaken for a slice of the Emerald Isle.

Always planning ahead, Jack and Anna Madden had purchased a cemetery plot next to their best friends, Mike and Ruth Tulley, several decades before they all died. And certainly, they had also made reservations to share a table at the heavenly banquet. The Madden plot was for five graves—Jack, Anna, my godmother Joan Marie, and my parents Frank and Joan. Divided into four equal sections, Frank and Joan would have to share one space dug a double depth to accommodate one casket buried atop the other. There were many playful jabs back and forth about which one of them would have to be underneath. And now we know. Though sharing the one grave seemed like a reasonable, cost-effective plan, the execution was a bit problematic since the casket on the bottom would have to be buried down extra deep.

I stopped into the office at St. Mary's Cemetery to chat with the director, Charles, about the grave.

"Hi, Charles. Can I talk to you about the Madden gravesite with the double-depth grave? My mother has passed away and will be the first one in that site. Um, can you explain how that works?"

"Well, you know we don't sell those kinds of plots anymore because we have too many headaches with them. We need to use a backhoe to lower the casket down into the grave because of the depth. If the ground is too soft, we run into problems with the backhoe."

"It might be disturbing to see a backhoe at the gravesite."

"Well, what we could do is keep the backhoe at the roadside until it is time for it. That way no one would really notice it."

"OK, yeah. That sounds better."

"If you have the Rite of Committal in the cemetery chapel then we can take care of everything afterwards. What we do then is have the backhoe lift the casket from the roadside, carry it fifty yards across the soft grass to the gravesite, and then lower it down seven feet."

At first, I had trouble picturing this in my mind. But then, I started thinking the worst. What if that didn't go as planned?

"That's quite the procedure. Do you ever have any mishaps?"

His answer wasn't very reassuring.

"No, not so far."

Later, I relayed this disturbing scenario to Mari and Ellyn. We agreed that it would be difficult to watch the casket maneuvered like that and if it didn't go well, even more difficult to erase the memory of it. So, we thought the best plan would be, as Charles suggested, to celebrate the Rite of Committal in the cemetery chapel and say our last goodbyes there.

Do Not Let Your Hearts Be Troubled.

"You have faith in God; have faith also in me.
In my Father's house there are many dwelling places.
If there were not,
would I have told you that I am going to prepare a place for you?
And if I go and prepare a place for you,
I will come back again and take you to myself, so that where I am you
also may be.
Where [I] am going you know the way."

Thomas said to him,
"Master, we do not know where you are going; how can we know the way?"
Jesus said to him,
"I am the way and the truth and the life."

(Jn 14:1-6a)

Chapter 14

The Rite of Committal

The Irish Blessing

May the road rise up to meet you
May the wind be always at your back
May the sun shine warm upon your face
And the rains fall softly on your fields
And until we meet again
May God hold you in the hollow of his hand.

We rode in procession to St. Mary's Cemetery and gathered in the chapel for the Rite of Committal. Deacon Kovach led the prayers that expressed our hope in the glory of the resurrection of mom and all those that have gone before us in faith. We prayed that she may be welcomed into the company of the saints and angels and all our family awaiting her arrival.[6]

As the rite came to an end, I sang the Irish blessing. With strains from my heart, I blessed mom's body and all those assembled, with the faith and the prayer of our ancestors in the hope that we will be together again one day.

Mari made the customary invitation for everyone to join us for lunch at Genetti's, the local favorite for large gatherings. The pain of leaving mom was softened by knowing that following this ritual we were headed toward another one.

It took a little bit more time for us to depart since Frank now required a wheelchair van with a professional driver to transport him. The van had a motorized liftgate that raised the wheelchair from ground level straight up to the rear of the vehicle so the wheelchair could be rolled right in. This was a new process for us and caused some anxiety, since Frank was a big man. He was proud of the fact that he was six feet six and a half inches tall, although not so proud that he now weighed north of three hundred pounds. The scary part was when the lift, acting as a cantilever, suspended Frank three feet above the ground until the wheelchair rolled into the van. Though it didn't seem to bother Frank in the least, we all held our breath until he was safely inside. By the time he was comfortably situated, everyone else had already gone on to the luncheon. Fortunately, Peter, Ellyn, and I were with Frank in the van because, as we drove past the graveside, we could see that the coffin had already been loaded onto the backhoe and was making its way toward the grave. Instinctively, I asked the driver to stop as close as possible. We sat in silence taking it all in. We didn't anticipate that we wouldn't be able to leave before her final procession was completed. Though we were physically distanced from mom, it felt as if a piece of us was going with her as she made her final passage. I was so grateful that we were with Frank to support him in this most heart-wrenching finale. He sat with quiet strength, watching, unmoving. His intense gaze seemed to be directing and controlling the entire operation. It was agonizing to watch Mrs. Hollywood's casket being carried by a backhoe, slowly inching across the grass to her gravesite. We watched and prayed until it was finished, until she was safely lowered into her final place of rest.

In Paradisum

May the Angels lead you into paradise;
may the Martyrs come to welcome you
and take you to the holy city,
the new and eternal Jerusalem.

Eternal rest grant unto her, O Lord,
and let perpetual light shine upon her.[7]
May the souls of the faithful departed,
through the mercy of God,
rest in peace.
Amen.

Chapter 15

The Fighting Irish in Overtime

Notre Dame Victory March

Cheer, cheer for old Notre Dame,
Wake up the echoes cheering her name,
Send a volley cheer on high,
Shake down the thunder from the sky.
What though the odds be great or small
Old Notre Dame will win over all,
While her loyal sons are marching
Onward to victory.

John F. Shea

Over one hundred people joined us for lunch at Genetti's. We had an open bar and a buffet of hand-carved roast beef, mashed potatoes, gravy, salad, mixed vegetables, and vegetarian pasta. Something for everyone. Though the stories about the wonderful impact mom had on people's lives continued, the attention started to become focused on Frank. Many people took me aside to ask what he was going to do now. Where would he live? Who would take care of him? Everyone knew that Frank had depended upon Joan for everything. Since Ellyn and I lived in California we wouldn't be able to help. Even though Mari and Jim lived nearby in Scranton, it was still a forty-five-minute drive away. Then, I overheard Aunt Nancy talking to Frank.

"Frank, how can Johnny and I help you now? This is not going to be easy."

"Nancy, I'll be fine. I am going to finish my rehab at Special Care Hospital and then I'll go back to the house. Don't worry about me. I'll be OK."

Keep at it, Riley! I have witnessed Frank's amazing ability to overcome all kinds of obstacles. But this was going to be quite a challenge. I had my doubts that he could pull this one off.

After the lunch concluded, we all went back to the house in Mountain Top. Maybe we didn't host a traditional Irish wake, but we certainly would do our best to throw a post-funeral celebration at the house. Sue, Paul, Mary, and David continued their meal ministry, making sure there was plenty out for everyone. The alcohol seemed to keep flowing from a well that never ran dry. In the Bible, Jesus turned water into wine at a wedding, but did he turn water into whiskey at a funeral? Well, it surely seemed as if the miracle was being performed on this day. But more important than all else, the lads had to get Frank up into the house. It was non-negotiable. He could not stay in the garage as he did the night before. No matter what the future might hold, this night Frank must be in the home he and his wife had built fifty years ago, gathered with his family and friends watching the Notre Dame football game on television.

Every entryway into the house had formidable steps but the fewest would be up the deck from the backyard. So, it took all the lads, sons-in-law, grandson, Wall nephews, and Foleys, to push Frank out the long driveway, across the front of the house on the street, up the neighbor's driveway, and over twenty yards of grass. After pulling Frank precariously in the wheelchair backwards up the three steps to the deck they were home free. Or so they thought, until they realized the extra-wide wheelchair couldn't fit through the sliding glass door. This was the toughest part, but no one gave up. Greg Wall, the volunteer firefighter, and Peter stood Frank up from the back as Jimmy Foley and Pat Wall guided him into the house from the front. Meanwhile, my son Greg, quickly snuck the wheelchair in through another door. As they hoisted Frank up, he loomed larger than all the lads, his face simultaneously mirroring pain and willpower. That would be the last time I ever saw dad upright.

Encircled by close family and friends Frank watched Notre Dame play Stanford, with his best friend, Uncle Johnny Wall, on his left and his high school buddy, Billy, on his right. Frank had cheered on the Irish all his life. The Fighting Irish Leprechaun was Frank's avatar, symbolizing his consistent stance of "Keep at it, Riley!" His undeniably proud Irish Catholic faith, evidenced by his special relationship with the Holy Cross priests at King's College, extended to the priests at Notre Dame. Whenever he had the chance, he would drive out to South Bend for a football game. He was even at the game when they filmed the movie, *Rudy*. Frank and Rudy had a lot in common—especially their unrelenting determination to never give up. Frank was probably shouting from the stands, "Keep at it, Rudy!"

That night, everyone in the house was cheering on the Fighting Irish and they needed it. Early in the game, ND scored a field goal but couldn't get the leather in the end zone again until the beginning of the fourth quarter, at last, tying up the score, 10 all. But Stanford quickly retaliated with a field goal and once again led the Irish 13-10. We screamed and we cheered until finally, in the last twenty seconds, ND gave us a twenty-two-yard field goal that tied the game and took us right into overtime! The luck of the Irish prevailed as Tommy Rees threw a seven-yard pass to T.J. Jones for a touchdown and the extra point easily followed. As if there never had been a doubt, the Notre Dame Fighting Irish won 20-13. We couldn't help but feel that we had our very own angel in heaven pulling for the Irish. Then, following the tradition after every Notre Dame game, win or lose, we wrapped our arms around each other, swayed side to side, and sang "Notre Dame, our Mother" as the Marching Band played on.

Unfortunately, Ellyn had to break up the party and get Frank back to Special Care Hospital. She could no longer ignore the pestering phone calls from the hospital. No doubt they were concerned; Frank himself was in overtime — two hours past his curfew.

As the lads retraced their steps to get Frank back down to the van, I couldn't help noticing that he had had more than a few drinks. I mentioned it to my children and the cousins.

"I wonder how Pop-Pop got overserved. He never moved from the TV."

Mollie confessed first, "Oh, I felt so bad for him, I gave him a whiskey."

Greg blurted out, "So did I!"

Then Kelley chimed in, "I gave him one too!"

Haley sheepishly said, "OK, I did too!"

"Well, that's four. Knowing our family, I'm sure there were a few more."

The entire drive back to the hospital, like a bad kid trying to make a good excuse to get out of trouble, Frank kept repeating the score and the final plays of the game to Ellyn. When they arrived, the director of nursing chewed them out for risking his health. And then escalated her objections when she noticed he'd been drinking. She argued that his temporary release was AMA, Against Medical Advice. It wasn't until Ellyn boldly raised her voice and snapped, "His wife just died!" that the nurse finally gave it a rest.

As Ellyn tucked Frank into bed, with genuine concern he said, "Your mother is going to be cold tonight."

Very soothingly Ellyn replied, "She is warm, Dad. She is with Jesus."

She was glad that it was too dark for him to see the tears rolling down her cheeks.

Notre Dame, our Mother, pray for us.

8

Notre Dame, Our Mother

Notre Dame, our Mother
Tender, strong and true
Proudly in the heavens,
Gleams the gold and blue.
Glory's mantle cloaks thee
Golden is thy fame
And our hearts forever
Praise thee, Notre Dame.
And our hearts forever,
Love thee, Notre Dame.

Charles L. O'Donnell, CSC

Chapter 16

The Little Flower

Red Is the Rose

Come over the hills, my bonnie Irish lass
Come over the hills to your darling
You choose the road, love, and I'll make the vow
And I'll be your true love forever

Red is the rose that in yonder garden grows
Fair is the lily of the valley
Clear is the water that flows from the Boyne
But my love is fairer than any

As I stepped through the front door of the nursing home, I was hit by the stench of urine and started to gag. Nauseated, I shook my head. "No. Oh, no. This place won't work. We can't let dad stay here. Let's go look at the next place on the list."

With tears in our eyes, we turned around, got back in the car, and went to the next skilled nursing facility on our list.

Mari, Ellyn, and I were desperate to find a living situation for Frank, since the short-term rehab hospital would be discharging him in only two weeks. Frank was determined to move back into his home in Mountain Top, but at this point he couldn't make it on his own, so we had to find a temporary solution. Though we had serious doubts that Frank would ever be able to go back to Mountain Top, we had seen this strong, stubborn, Irishman bounce back from illnesses before and maybe he could this time too. But without mom it was going to be much harder. We felt that it wasn't our place to tell him he couldn't do it, nor should we even discourage him from trying. It was our job to support him and help him realize his dream. We started scoping out his options so he could make an informed decision about where he could live temporarily while he regained his strength.

Health care facilities offer several tiers of assistance, ranging from independent living to 24/7 care nursing units. "Independent living" allows you to have your own private apartment with resources conveniently available as needed. "Assisted living" offers your own space with minimal intervention for supervision and support. "In-patient rehabilitation centers" are typically short-term care facilities that provide twenty-four-hour transitional care before going back home after a hospital stay, the kind of center that Frank was currently in. What we had always called "convalescent homes," or "nursing homes," are now referred to as "skilled nursing facilities" or SNFs. A SNF provides twenty-four-hour skilled care for assistance with several activities of daily living (ADL): bathing, eating, dressing, toileting, transferring, and walking.

I recalled my friend Julie telling me that her parents had moved to a continuing care retirement community, a senior living compound that offered all levels of care on one campus. The benefit was the possibility to transfer easily from one level to another as needed. I called Julie to let her know what had happened to my mom, and to see how the retirement community was working out for her family.

"Julie, I have sad news. My mom passed away suddenly in a car accident."

"Oh, Noreen, that's terrible. I'm so sorry about your mom. She was such a great lady."

I filled Julie in on our dilemma, "And now, my dad can't live on his own. We have been looking for a living situation for him, and I was wondering how the retirement community was working out for your parents."

Julie tenderly replied, "This is such a difficult time for your family. I hope you find the right situation for your dad. But unfortunately, I can't say that the retirement community has panned out as well as we had hoped."

"Julie, I'm surprised to hear that. They always market these places like you would be living next door to the sexy old guy that looks like Paul Newman and the hilarious senior socialite like Betty White. What's going on?"

"Well, in the beginning it was great. My parents acted like a couple of newlyweds vacationing at Club Med. They hit all the restaurants on campus; hung out at the bars; played tennis; worked out in the gym. They made lots of new friends. . . Not exactly Paul Newman and Betty White, but pretty darn close. They traveled quite a bit, too, since it was easy to pick up and go without the responsibility of taking care of their home."

Laughing, I said, "That all sounds amazing! Sign me up!"

Julie continued, "Yeah, it really was great until my parents started to decline. My father took a nasty spill that sent him from their independent living apartment to the hospital. When he was discharged, he needed some rehab to get back on his feet, so he went to the SNF on campus. It seemed reasonable, but six weeks later he was still in the SNF. It's hard for me to get to the Midwest from California so I was trying to manage it over the phone. I couldn't get a reasonable explanation for why dad wasn't going back home, and my mother didn't seem to have a clue. So, I finally got on a plane to check it out for myself."

I could totally relate to the challenge with distance and commiserated, "It's really frustrating being so far away."

"Yes, frustrating, but worse than that, what I found was depressing. I discovered that my dad was placed on the dementia floor of the SNF. All the patients in the unit had severe memory issues. Now, it was good to know that this option was available when it was needed, but my dad didn't have dementia. Well, at least six weeks ago he didn't. But now it appeared that my father didn't really know where he was, and at times who he was. He was in such a state of confusion that he actually appeared to have dementia."

"Oh, that's terrible. What did you do?"

"My first inclination was to just get him out of there and back to the independent living situation. But in order to do that I had to hire an aide to assist dad with some of his ADLs. The bizarre thing was that my mother was opposed to it because she didn't want someone coming into their apartment. She didn't seem to understand that this was the only way he could return home. But I made the arrangements and convinced mom that it would be cheaper than staying in the SNF. That seemed to work, since money always weighed heavily in my parents' decision making."

I was all too familiar with that. "Yes of course. Many elderly have a lot of anxiety about running out of money and becoming dependent upon their children."

Julie confided, "It was great to get dad back into his apartment, but even better when he got off the medications he was on in the SNF. He was his old self again. It became obvious that he was overly medicated on the dementia floor."

"Oh Julie, I am so sorry. That's terrible."

Julie admitted, "I am sorry for my parents too. They thought they had done a good job getting their living situation all sorted out by moving into a good retirement community that would accompany them as they aged. But without an advocate nearby the elderly can easily be taken advantage of."

"Oh, Julie, this is so sad. I hope your parents are doing better now."

"Yes, much better. And I make it a point to visit more regularly. I really need to see first-hand how they are doing."

"Julie, thank you for sharing your story. It helps to know that the continuing care retirement community isn't always the best answer. It's just as well since my dad would have to move out of Mountain Top to be in one since there aren't any in the area. And he has made it crystal clear that he wants no part of moving."

I hung up the phone with a lot on my mind. It seemed that the only option for Frank was a SNF since right now he needed assistance with all the ADLs except for feeding himself. Further complicating the situation was finding a SNF that had an open bed in just two weeks. My sisters and I made our list and started checking them out, one by one.

The typical SNFs we toured were nursing homes for seniors. It broke our hearts to see so many elderly patients in various states of physical and mental debility. The overworked, understaffed caregivers could not possibly provide all the attention their patients needed and deserved. Many of the patients were bedridden and completely dependent upon the staff for all their bodily needs. It wasn't quite clear how their spiritual and social needs would be met. An overwhelming sense of doom and gloom hung in the air, seemingly sucking the life right out of everyone. Many of the residents were designated Do Not Resuscitate (DNR), which allows a person to pass naturally without any heroic or futile medical intervention. With a DNR, the residents still receive all necessary medical treatment, but if they were to pass naturally, the staff would not intervene.

Dr. Charles Camosy, professor of theological and social ethics, explains that Catholic teaching demands that one should never aim at the death of an innocent person even by omission. However, one can withhold medical treatment if it can be reasonably determined that the burden of its administration is disproportionate with respect to any expected benefit.[9] For example, someone suffering from terminal disease may consider cardiopulmonary resuscitation (CPR) to be burdensome. Brigham and Women's Faulkner Hospital clarifies that "[CPR] uses mouth-to-mouth or machine breathing and chest compressions to restore the work of the heart and lungs when someone's heart or breathing has stopped. It is an emergency rescue technique that was developed to save the life of people who are generally in good health."[10] Admittedly, DNR was the chosen option for most of the patients in these facilities. This was their last stop. In other words, their only way out of the SNF was in a body bag.

The year before, Frank had a bout of illness that required the regular rotation from the hospital, to rehab, to home. But since there were no rehab centers nearby with available beds, he had to go to a SNF instead. These transitions were difficult for mom. Making decisions about choosing health care facilities was overwhelming and wearing her down. Frank knew that mom wouldn't be able to handle one more challenge, so in desperation he called me.

As the phone rang, I picked it up and Frank whispered, in a weak voice,

"Noreen, get me out of here."

"Dad, what's wrong?"

"I feel like I'm in a concentration camp."

"Oh, no. What's going on?"

"I was on the toilet for two hours this morning."

"You, what?"

"I rang for help to get to the toilet, and that was fine, but then they left me there. I kept ringing and ringing for someone to help me back to bed, but no one came for two hours."

"Oh, Dad. I'm so sorry."

"I asked for water, and they told me I have to wait for mealtimes. They said they can't be running in and out of every room all day long. And, yesterday, I asked to be taken to the toilet, and they didn't come for an hour. So, as you can imagine that, by then, it wasn't the toilet I needed but a diaper change."

"Oh, Dad. I can't believe how cruel this is."

"I know. I think I'm the only patient here that knows what's going on, so they think they can get away with this."

It just tore my heart out to be three thousand miles away from my dad in situations like this. After a series of phone calls, we got him moved out of the "concentration camp" into a rehab facility with much better care. That's when we made a vow to never let Frank in a place like that, ever again.

Mari, Ellyn, and I continued to make our way down the list, crossing them off one by one for varying reasons. The stench of urine, of course, was the tell-tale sign that the patients were being left in soiled diapers. Not only did we want to keep Frank out of that kind of place, but we also couldn't think about anyone living that way. We wanted to take them all home with us, until we got to Little Flower Manor. Opening the front door, we passed by a crucifix as we made our way down the hallway to Sister Maureen's office. Just seeing her in the familiar Carmelite brown habit made my heart melt. I knew right away this was an answer to our prayers. Little Flower, owned by the Roman Catholic Diocese of Scranton, was a long-term health care facility run by Carmelite Sisters. Sister Maureen assured us that

Frank would be well cared for there. He could receive daily Communion in his room and attend Mass in the chapel as he was able. Hope in the resurrection replaced the doom and gloom we sensed in the other SNFs. Here, a DNR meant that this is God's waiting room, the threshold of heaven. This wasn't the last stop. The best was yet to come, not just a body bag. The angels will come to take us home to God.

> What eye has not seen, and ear has not heard,
> and what has not entered the human heart,
> what God has prepared for those who love him.

(1 Cor 2:9)

I felt my eyes well up as Sister Maureen told us that there was a room available, next door to a monsignor and across the hall from a sister. Now, we were ready to talk to Frank.

"Dad, Special Care Hospital will be discharging you in a couple of weeks."

Frank, with his typical determination, had it all figured out and no matter the odds was going to make it happen. "I'm going back to my own house. I am going to get back on my feet again and I'll be fine on my own."

"That sounds really good, Dad. So, you need a place to help you get back on your feet again?"

"Yeah, that's it. Then, I am going back to Mountain Top."

"All right. Well, we looked at a few places and the best one we found was Little Flower Manor. You can get daily Communion there and Dr. D. stops by once a week to see his patients. How does that sound?"

"Would I have my own room and bathroom?"

"Yes, you would."

"All right, then. But just until I get back on my feet."

"OK, Dad."

We stopped into Dr. D.'s office to chat with him about Frank's situation.

"Dr. D., Frank will be going to Little Flower Manor after he's discharged from Special Care."

"That's a good place. I can still see him there."

"What is your assessment of Frank's health at this point?"

"You know your father is very fragile; he suffers from several serious medical ailments. He was in a delicate situation before your mother's death, and now this has dealt him a terrible blow. I'm sure you have heard of the widower effect; couples that have been married many years often closely follow each other in death."

Nodding my head, I replied, "I understand. Frank says he wants to get back on his feet and move back to his house in Mountain Top."

Dr. D. sighed, "Well, he is very weak right now."

I stood my ground. "You know he's determined. Little Flower has a nice rehab facility. The opportunity is there for him to give it a try. We need to honor his decision, his wishes."

"That sounds good. I'll do all I can on my end to take good care of him."

"That is sincerely appreciated, doctor. Thank you for all you do."

It was truly heart wrenching when the time came for Ellyn and me to say good-bye to dad and return to California. He was without mom. He couldn't walk. Yet, we were comforted knowing that he would be well cared for by the Carmelite sisters. Would dad get back on his feet? It didn't seem likely, but we had seen him recover before. He's made of tough stuff. He's in God's hands.

Prayer of St. Thérèse of Lisieux, "The Little Flower"

May today there be peace within.
May you trust God that you are exactly
where you are meant to be.
May you not forget the infinite possibilities
that are born of faith.
May you use those gifts that you have received,
and pass on the love that has been given to you.
May you be content knowing you are a child of God.
Let this presence settle into your bones,
and allow your soul the freedom to sing, dance,
praise, and love.
It is there for each and every one of us.

Chapter 17

The Visitation

Daisy A Day

I'll give you a daisy a day dear
I'll give you a daisy a day
I'll love you until the rivers run still
And the four winds we know blow away.

Now he walks down the street in the evenin'
And he stops by the old candy store
And I somehow believe he's believin'
He's holdin' 'er hand like before.
For he feels all her love walkin' with him
And he smiles at the things she might say
Then the old man walks up to the hilltop
And gives her a daisy a day.

Jud Strunk

Frank got moved into Little Flower and started to settle into their routine. I continued my daily phone call, aka, "The Telephone Medical Diagnostic System," "Dad, how's it going?"

"Pretty good."

He was famous for his "pretty good" answer. He didn't really complain much. But in order to find out what was actually going on, I had to ask specific questions.

"How's the food?"

"Well, better now."

Confused, I asked, "What do you mean, better now?"

"Like most of these places they were overcooking their meat. But I straightened them out."

"Oh no. What did you do now?"

"I called the kitchen and told them how I like my meat cooked. That's all."

"Dad, be careful. Remember when they told you at Special Care Hospital that you weren't allowed to call the kitchen anymore? They said they weren't running a restaurant."

"Oh, it wasn't that bad. They were actually very appreciative when I called the facilities office to report the clogged drain in the shower."

"Dad, you are something."

"Well, I won't bother the kitchen too much more. I'm bringing them up to speed one issue at a time. I'll probably stop after I get them on board with sending me two desserts instead of only one."

Laughing, I scolded, "We are going to get an extra food bill for you."

"Well, I'm worth it."

"And yes, you are!" I laughed at his mischievous nature and could just picture the twinkle in his eye.

"Dad, Ellyn and I are coming to visit you in a couple of weeks. Is there anything you need?"

"No. The only thing I need is to see your faces. That would be great!"

Two weeks later, Ellyn and I flew across the country, she from Sacramento and I from San Diego, and met at the Philadelphia airport to start the final leg up to Mountain Top. Before we got on the road, Ellyn decided that we needed to pick up a Philly Cheesesteak hoagie for dad. What could be better to cheer up Frank than the traditional crusty Italian roll, filled with thinly sliced grilled beef and onions and

Cheez Whiz drizzled all over the top? This would certainly brighten up our foodie father! Though Ellyn and I easily agreed on the cheesesteak, we didn't immediately agree on the best place to buy it. Should it be Geno's or Pat's? This perennial dispute among the Philadelphia locals will never be resolved. There were generations of followers for Geno and just as many disciples of Pat but crossing over could cause a gang war. Nonetheless, we came to the conclusion that we really couldn't go wrong; either one would lift Frank's spirits. Two hours later, we arrived at Little Flower, so proud to offer him the iconic heavenly delight on a bun. Unfortunately, it didn't work the magic that we hoped for. We probably should have seen that as a red flag. He was happy just to be with us. Obviously, we were his treat.

That night, before going to sleep in our parents' empty home, we stopped at Cavanaugh's for a shot of courage. Kevin was there to welcome us with a round of drinks. I was happy to have the local favorite on tap, Yuengling, but Ellyn needed something a little sweeter and a lot stronger. Annie brought Ellyn her favorite, a birdbath of Bailey's Irish Cream on the rocks. It certainly helped blot out the pain from losing mom and seeing Frank in such misery. And if that one didn't do it, the third one did for sure.

The next day we were grateful that we could accompany Frank to the Sunday morning Mass in the Little Flower chapel. Dressed in our Sunday best we wheeled him down to join the fifty or so other residents gathered to celebrate the Eucharist. After the homily, I couldn't help noticing that about ninety percent of the residents were sound asleep, sawing wood, conked out, not even head-bobbing. To be honest, the homily really wasn't that bad. So why were they all deep in la-la land with their chins lying on their chests? It is too much of a coincidence that so many of them were out of it? Should we start to question whether they were all medicated? Oh, I'm not sure I want to go down that path. Frank was wide awake and so was a section of priests sitting up in the right front pews. Somehow, Frank seemed unruffled by all this.

After Mass, Ellyn went up to one of the priests from the "wide-awake section."

"Aren't you Monsignor Clark? My mom was Joan Madden from North End. I think you taught her at College Misericordia."

"Why, yes. I did, and as a matter of fact, she stops in to visit me here often."

Like ripping off a band-aid, Ellyn broke the news, "I'm sorry to tell you that Joan passed away suddenly one month ago."

"Oh, I'm so sorry to hear that. She was a wonderful woman, and the best student I ever had."

"Monsignor, this is my father, Frank, and my sister, Noreen. Frank moved into Little flower a couple of weeks ago."

"Welcome. It's so nice to meet you. Say, I live in an apartment here at Little Flower, in the independent living section, would you all like to come up for a coffee?"

We all went up and squeezed into Monsignor Clark's modest apartment. His warm hospitality and the stories of mom from her college days were so soothing. Just what we needed. Then, Monsignor told us he was turning ninety soon and wasn't sure why he was still around. All of his friends and colleagues were gone. He said sadly, "Maybe God has forgotten about me."

Ellyn replied, "Well, you know our mom always said that the angels won't come to take you to up to heaven until your work is done. So, God must have something more for you to do here."

It was such a comfort to be with Monsignor Clark. Maybe our little visit with him was part of the work he still had to do. And I wondered if Frank had more to do before the angels came for him.

When it came time for Ellyn and me to return to our families in California, we smiled and hugged Frank cheerfully. But as soon as we left his room, the sobs came, and came, and kept on coming. It hurt so bad to leave him. We left a big piece of our hearts with Frank at Little Flower.

The Visitation

During those days Mary set out and traveled to the hill country
in haste to a town of Judah,
where she entered the house of Zechariah and greeted Elizabeth.
When Elizabeth heard Mary's greeting,
the infant leaped in her womb,
and Elizabeth, filled with the holy Spirit,
cried out in a loud voice and said,
"Most blessed are you among women,
and blessed is the fruit of your womb.
And how does this happen to me,
that the mother of my Lord should come to me?
For at the moment the sound of your greeting reached my ears,
the infant in my womb leaped for joy.
Blessed are you who believed
that what was spoken to you by the Lord would be fulfilled."

(Lk 1:39-45)

Chapter 18

The Call

Call me when you're ready, Lord.
And, Lord, make me ready when you call me.

Rev. Msgr. Lloyd Bourgeois

E arly Sunday morning, at home in San Diego, I sat at my piano rehearsing the responsorial psalm for the day's Mass, the Second Sunday of Advent, Year C. As the cantor, I had been asked to lead the assembly singing Psalm 126: "The Lord has done great things for us, we are filled with joy."

Suddenly the phone rang, abruptly interrupting my prayerful preparation.

"Hello, Noreen?

"Yes, this is Noreen."

"This is Dr. D. I'm, I'm so sorry to tell you this, but your father is dying. His vital signs are not looking good, and he is not responding to any medications."

Though I had rehearsed this moment in my head so many times, it didn't help one bit.

"Oh, no!

"Yes, we moved Frank back to Special Care Hospital when his vital signs dropped two days ago, but he has been going steadily downhill ever since."

"Thank you so much for calling me. I'll get there as quickly as I can."

I was shocked, frozen. I felt helpless at hearing this news. What do I do first?

I was the only one at home that morning. Peter was in Germany on a business trip. Greg was at his home in nearby Pacific Beach. Kelley was living in Seattle. Mollie was sleeping over at a friend's house. And thanks be to God, our friend Chris, who used to be in the choir with us at St. John's, just always seemed to be fifteen minutes away whenever we needed him.

As if by divine inspiration, the phone rang again. It was Peter, calling from Germany to check in.

He could hear the sadness in my voice. "Hi honey, I'm so glad you called. I got a call that Frank is dying. I'm supposed to be the cantor at Mass in an hour. What should I do?"

"Go to Mass. Sing the psalm. Then go to Mountain Top."

That was all I needed to shake off the paralysis and get myself focused. Kelley, with her great planning skills, would be the one to figure out how to fly to Mountain Top on such short notice.

"Kelley, Pop-Pop, is not doing well. I need to get to Mountain Top right away. Can you make travel arrangements for me to get there today? Here is my credit card number, arrange whatever you think is best."

"Got it, mom."

"Greg, Pop-Pop, is not doing well. I need to get to Mountain Top right away. Can you come home and stay with Mollie here at the house while I go to Mountain Top?"

"Sure. No problem."

"Mollie, Pop-Pop, is not doing well. I need to get to Mountain Top right away. Can you come home and help me pack?"

"OK."

"Thanks, honey. Can you get a ride home and meet me here at 10:15?"

"Yeah, see you then."

"Chris, Frank, is not doing well. I need to get to Mountain Top right away. It's not good."

"I'll be there in fifteen minutes."

"OK. Well, I'm running to Mass right now. I'll be back at 10:15."

I walked into the church just as I had so many times before over the last twenty-five years. The familiar crucifix hanging behind the altar met my eye and drew me in. Through the image of the suffering Jesus on the cross I felt a warm embrace of God's love outpoured.

Then it hit me. How can I possibly sing this psalm, "The Lord has done great things for us; we are filled with joy" while knowing my father is dying? I looked back at the crucifix, as if seeing it for the first time. I saw Jesus dying on the cross, undergoing the agony of his impending death.

"Please, Jesus, be with my father, be his comfort, as he is dying."

"Blessed Mother, intercede for me, that I will be able to accompany my father through this trial. Just as you stood at the foot of the cross as your son died, give me the strength to stand beside my dad as he dies. Please, let me get there in time to be with him."

As Mass began, I was reminded that we were celebrating the Paschal Mystery, the suffering, death, and resurrection of Jesus. He surrendered his will for the will of the Father so that "dying, he destroyed our death and, rising, he restored our life."[11]

So, "Where, O death, is your sting?" (1 Cor 15:55b). Through Christ Jesus, life is changed, not ended. We are not dying but entering into eternal life.[12] And that was the reason I could sing with all my heart that "the Lord has done great things for us; we are filled with joy."

> The Lord has done great things for us;
> we are filled with joy.
> When the LORD brought back the captives of Zion,
> we were like men dreaming.
> Then our mouth was filled with laughter,
> and our tongue with rejoicing.
>
> Then they said among the nations,
> "The LORD has done great things for them."
> The LORD has done great things for us;
> we are glad indeed.
>
> Restore our fortunes, O LORD,
> like the torrents in the southern desert.
> Those who sow in tears
> shall reap rejoicing.
>
> Although they go forth weeping,
> carrying the seed to be sown,
> They shall come back rejoicing,
> carrying their sheaves.
>
> (Ps 126: 1-2, 2-3, 4-5, 6)

Just after I sang the responsorial psalm, I got a text from Kelley with the perfect itinerary. I had just enough time to get home, speed-pack with Mollie's help and get to the airport. I left Mass; Mollie packed for me; Greg walked in the door. Hugs and prayers all around and I'm on my way! I am so grateful for my faith and my loving family. Chris drove me to the airport and just before I stepped out of the car, he handed me a stack of free drink coupons for the flight.

I made the long trip to Mountain Top praying non-stop rosaries all along the way. I finally arrived at my father's bedside, holding my breath, not sure what I would find. I peered over him closely, searching for signs of breathing.

Frank opened his eyes to let me take in the bluest blue eyes one has ever seen.

He said, "Oh! Hi!" and quietly smiled.

And from that moment on, he began to recover.

Sigh!

Anima Christi

Soul of Christ, sanctify me.
Body of Christ, save me.
Blood of Christ, inebriate me.
Water from the side of Christ, wash me.
Passion of Christ, strengthen me.
O good Jesus, hear me.
Within your wounds hide me.
Permit me not to be separated from you.
From the wicked foe, defend me.
At the hour of my death, call me
and bid me come to you
That with your saints
and with your angels
I may praise you
For ever and ever.
Amen.

St. Ignatius of Loyola

Chapter 19

Ronald

I see Jesus in every human being.
I say to myself; this is hungry Jesus; I must feed him.
This is sick Jesus.
This one has leprosy or gangrene;
I must wash him and tend to him.
I serve because I love Jesus.

St. Teresa of Calcutta

Early the next morning, right after Mass at St. Jude's, I walked into dad's hospital room to find him sitting up in a chair, finishing his breakfast. The nurse popped her head into the room and asked,

"Frank, are you ready to go back down to rehab today?"

"Sure, I'll give it a try."

I was speechless. Yesterday, he was dying, today, he is all full of optimism, ready to go to rehabilitation to get back on his feet.

"Dad, do you mind if I go to rehab with you?"

"No, that would be great, you can take me down there!"

After he got cleaned up from breakfast, I pushed dad in his wheelchair down to the large rehab room in the basement. As I walked in, my knees started to buckle from under me.

I looked from face to face at all the blank stares on the patients parked around the room. Not one of them seemed to know where they were, let alone who they were. I wanted to turn my dad right around and run out of there. He didn't belong here. The rehab therapist pointed to an empty spot along the wall where she wanted dad to go. Oh, no, not there. That was right next to the scariest one of them all. He was sitting in his wheelchair, moving erratically, his opened hospital gown displaying his catheter. His urine bag hung on one side of his chair and an IV pole with a drip into his arm on the other. Though seemingly much younger than all the other patients, this guy was definitely more out of it. He was completely staring into space. I was nervous, scared, and uncomfortable. I couldn't look at that urine bag.

I did as I was told and backed Frank into the spot next to the urine bag, when the young man screamed out with great energy and fervor, "Frrrraaaaannnnk!!!!!"

Frank turned, smiled, and, in a sing-song-voice, called out, "Well hello, Ronald."

Ronald yelled even louder, "Frrrraaaaannnnk!!!!!"

The rehab therapist leaned in and whispered, "Ronald has been here for three months now and in that time, he has only said one word—'Frank'!"

What did I know? I tried to look around the room with new eyes, but I was still traumatized. My gaze stopped at a woman, drooling and hunched over in her chair. Before I knew it, Frank looked right at her and said in a flirtatious voice,

"Hi there, Maureen."

The drooling face turned toward Frank, ever so slightly, and I caught a glimpse of the slow, sexy wink aimed right at Frank. The whole place erupted in laughter.

Was Frank here for himself? Was he the patient, or was he sent here to heal those around him? Obviously, God was in control here. I could no longer look with aversion or fear but only with love and compassion for these children of God. My father taught me more in those five minutes than I learned in six years at Notre Dame studying liturgy. He taught me to see Jesus in the sick and the suffering.

The Parable of the Good Samaritan

"Who is my neighbor?"
Jesus replied,
"A man fell victim to robbers as he went down
from Jerusalem to Jericho.
They stripped and beat him and went off
leaving him half-dead.
A priest happened to be going down that road,
but when he saw him, he passed by
on the opposite side.
Likewise a Levite came to the place,
and when he saw him, he passed by
on the opposite side.
But a Samaritan traveler who came upon him
was moved with compassion at the sight.
He approached the victim,
poured oil and wine over his wounds
and bandaged them.
Then he lifted him up on his own animal,
took him to an inn and cared for him.
The next day he took out two silver coins
and gave them to the innkeeper with the instruction,
'Take care of him. If you spend more than what
I have given you,
I shall repay you on my way back.'
Which of these three, in your opinion, was neighbor
to the robbers' victim?"
He answered, "The one who treated him with mercy."
Jesus said to him, "Go and do likewise."

(Lk 10:29-37)

Chapter 20

The Flying Coffin

So we are always courageous,
although we know that while
we are at home in the body
we are away from the Lord,
for we walk by faith, not by sight.
Yet we are courageous,
and we would rather leave the body
and go home to the Lord.

(2 Cor 5:6-8)

Frank improved steadily each day. One by one, each of his nurses pulled me aside and whispered, "You need to stay here in Pennsylvania. Frank is doing so much better now that you are with him."

With a sad heart I replied, "I wish I could stay here but I have a husband and children in California."

Lord, help me. What do I do? My heart was aching, no, it was breaking! I had been on such an emotional roller coaster over the last couple of days. I left the hospital and drove to the cemetery where my mother had been buried only two months before. I stood over her fresh grave, tears streaming into the ground where my mother's body lay, resting in peace. I knelt down upon the grass that covered the graves of my mother, my godmother, and my grandparents. As my tears descended into the soil my prayers rose up into the heavens.

Through my sobs and trembling lips, I helplessly muttered to them, "I don't have any answers, but I think you might. You are surely in heaven. You lived amazing God-centered lives and now we desperately need your advice. Tell me, how do I care for your husband, your brother, your son? I need your intervention. Please, help us. And do it quickly."

Led by some unseen angel, I returned to the hospital, to my father's side.

I heard the words pour out of my mouth. "Dad, come to California! We can take good care of you there." I extended the invitation confidently, as if I had it all thought through. Hell, no! Not even close.

Dad shook his head vehemently, "Noreen, I promised myself years ago, I would never be a burden to any of my daughters."

I teased him, "But you don't have to break that promise, because you wouldn't be a burden."

He sternly recoiled, "The answer is no and that's that. It's final. End of discussion."

Now, my Irish was up, "Yeah, well, I can tell that you are Irish, because I can't tell you anything."

I had him there. The backhanded compliment called him out. He was clinging tightly to his promise like only the Irish can hold onto a grudge. And we all know that doesn't do anybody any good.

I spent a quiet night in the painfully empty house of my parents with my Jameson and my rosary. The next morning, I made my way to Mass at St. Jude's, settling my knees down into my mother's worn-in kneeler. After Mass, I made the usual rounds, praying before her statues, and checking on her candle. As I left the church, I found a message from dad on my phone.

"Noreen, I made my mind up, I'm coming. Are you sure? This is a big undertaking. I'm a cripple. But I've decided to come. I hope that's OK. I'm coming."

I closed my eyes and exhaled deeply. Praise the Lord! My fervent prayers had been answered. Uh, oh. Oh, dear. I need to talk to Peter. We had talked generally about the possibility of Frank coming to live with us. I knew that Peter was open to the idea, but we had never really come to a definitive agreement. And as Frank's message stated, it would be a big undertaking. I had to call Peter right away.

"Hi honey."

"Good morning, my love."

"Good morning."

"How's everything going?"

Getting right to the point I asked, "Um, would it be OK if my father comes to live with us?"

My husband, the un-canonized saint, said, "YES!"

Time would reveal just how much of a saint Peter really is. This was only the beginning! Was I crazy? Or was I being guided by my angel, or by Frank's angel? or by the combined forces of the angels of my mother, godmother, and grandparents who obviously answered my prayers?

Now that the decision had been made, we had to mobilize and put a plan into action.

The first question was, how do we get Frank clear across the continent? Frank weighed 350 pounds, stood 6' 6," yet couldn't walk or even stand on his own. Hmm. . . I had to consult with Ellyn about this.

"Ellyn, are you sitting down?"

"Yeah. . . OK now I am. Go ahead."

"Dad agreed to move to San Diego!"

"That's amazing news! So, now we have to figure out how to get him there."

"Exactly. I don't think dad can take a commercial flight from Philadelphia to San Diego. Even if it's non-stop."

Ellyn said, "He was recently fitted with a catheter, so he won't have to worry about using the rest room for urinating. But we would still have to worry about other bathroom needs in mid-flight."

"Well, let's back up. How will he transfer from a wheelchair to the seat on the airplane without a Hoyer lift? Because of his size, every transfer from a wheelchair to another seat has to be done with a hydraulic lift and a sling underneath to lift and move him."

"Yeah, I can't see that happening on a commercial flight."

As we were speaking I was searching madly through various medical transportation websites. . . then there it was. "Ellyn, wait a minute. I just found a medevac flight on the internet. It's a private flight that's like an air ambulance."

"OK, that sounds like the way to go. Ask dad what he thinks."

I walked into dad's hospital room, so happy to be springing him out of there. Though he received excellent care, it wasn't home. Now, to begin working out the logistics, I gently broached the subject,

"Dad, I think flying commercially to San Diego would be quite a hassle. We would have to get you down to Philadelphia, onto the flight, and then fly across the country. I just think that sounds like too much. But I found a private medevac flight that could work. It could take you straight from here across the country with medical professionals on board. How does that sound?"

"What kind of plane would it be?"

"They use a Learjet."

"You mean those small planes? You know what they call those don't you?"

"No, what?"

"They call them flying coffins. You could die in those things."

Seriously? This man, who has been near death countless times, had had the anointing of the sick as many times as I have fingers, was now afraid of flying in a small plane?

I simply replied, "OK. Gotcha. I'll figure something else out."

I went back out into the hallway and started scouring the internet for plan "B" on my phone. Hmm. . . . What's this medical coach?

I gave them a quick call then checked with Ellyn to see what she thought.

"Ellyn, what about a medical coach? It's a long-distance non-emergency medical transport in an RV. I called them and they can send out the McDonald twins, one drives while the other sleeps. They claim they can make it across the country in forty-eight hours, door to door. And there is a nurse that rides with them too. Does this make sense?"

Ellyn said, "Wow. That sounds amazing. See what dad thinks about this."

"OK, I'll let you know."

I walked back into dad's room and made the pitch for the medical coach scenario.

"Noreen, that sounds pretty good to me. But how much does that cost?"

Lying through my teeth, for the first and only time, I told him, "Don't worry about the cost, Dad. I have that all worked out. So, should we set it up?"

"All right. Let's do it. Go tell Dr. D. that I am going to California. Ask him to set up the discharge plan and whatever else we need from him."

I went down the hall to Dr. D.'s office, praying as I walked.

"Hi Dr. D."

"Hi," he responded. "Frank's recovery is truly remarkable. Only three days ago I called to tell you that he was dying and now he has bounced back and is even doing rehab again."

"Yes. Well, his motto has always been, 'Keep at it, Riley!' and this is just one more example of how he operates. As a matter of fact, Frank would like to move to California."

"What do you mean?"

"He is going to move in with me and my family in San Diego."

"How would he get there?"

"I have a medical coach lined up that will transport him door to door."

"I am sorry to disappoint you, but I cannot approve of this. Your father's health is fragile and it's very likely that he won't survive the trip. Even if he does, you will probably end up in an emergency room halfway across the country and then what will you do?"

"OK. I understand. Well, if you don't mind, can we talk with Frank about this?"

I walked back into Frank's room with Dr. D.

Dr. D. blurted out, rather sternly, "Frank, I'm sorry but I have to say that I cannot give you my blessing to move to California. It's what we call AMA, Against Medical Advice. You are too fragile to make the trip."

Dad looked at me quizzically and started laughing.

"What do you know? He thinks I'm fragile!"

Now I was laughing. All his life, Frank had been as strong as a bull; he was a mountain of a man. So, hearing that he was fragile, cracked us up.

Knowing this was a pivotal moment, I said, "Well, Dr. D. has a point. The trip could be rough on you. Are you sure you want to go for it?"

"Absolutely, I do." And laughing, he added, "Even if I'm fragile."

Later, when dad was out of earshot, I called Ellyn.

"Ellyn, Dr. D. says he is not in favor of dad travelling to California. It's AMA. What do you think?"

"Dad wants to go, right?"

"Right!"

"He was not doing well on his own, right?"

"Right!"

"Then I think we should support his wishes as best we can."

"Agreed."

We would remind ourselves of this interchange more than once as we struggled with the details to make the trip happen. With that decided, we agreed that I would go back to San Diego to prepare for Frank's arrival while Ellyn would come to Mountain Top with her husband, Andy, to pack up whatever dad needed. Ellyn would then ride with him on the medical coach to San Diego. California here we come!

Prayer of St. Brendan the Navigator
Irish Patron of Sailors

Help me to journey beyond the familiar
and into the unknown.
Give me the faith to leave old ways
and break fresh ground with You.
Christ of the mysteries, I trust You
to be stronger than each storm within me.
I will trust in the darkness and know
that my times, even now, are in Your hand.
Tune my spirit to the music of heaven,
and somehow, make my obedience count for You.
Amen.

Chapter 21

The American Wake

Bread of Angels

Panis angelicus
Fit panis hominum
Dat panis coelicus
Figuris terminum
O res mirabilis
Manducat dominum
Pauper, pauper
Servus et humilis

St. Thomas Aquinas

W hat inspired the Irish to leave a country they held so dear and travel dangerously to an unknown land? During the Great Famine, some felt a compulsion to escape, yet others remained behind. Is it the fight or flight instinct that kicks in when one faces a crisis? Must you have a tremendous sense of desperation to risk a move? The Irish that fled the famine definitely took a chance. They traveled to America aboard sailing vessels they called coffin ships because the death rates onboard were as high as thirty percent. Sharks were said to follow them, feeding on the dead thrown overboard. Overcrowding and unsanitary conditions were the norm. The height between the passenger decks could be as little as four feet, with four strangers sharing berths just six feet square. The hay-lined wooden-slatted berths, stacked in tiers, allowed bodily fluids to flow onto those below. The close quarters provided a breeding ground for typhoid and lice. Since the voyage could last anywhere from thirty days to three months, food and clean water were often in short supply.[13]

The sendoff for those bound for America, never to be seen again, came to be known as the "American Wake." As health and funds allowed, family and friends danced and sang, drank and smoked, until they walked the emigrants down to the ship and saw them off. Their strong faith in the resurrection of the dead changed a final good-bye to "until we meet again." They lined the shore to watch the ship disappear over the horizon, sailing toward a distant land. Though separated by distance or death, their baptism, and continued prayers for each other bound them together as one body in Christ.

When Frank's men's group learned that he would soon be moving to California, they gathered at Special Care Hospital to celebrate their "California Wake." The six St. Jude's men who had supported each other for decades met one last time in prayer, laughter, and love. Joe Baltz, who had been a minister of Holy Communion to Frank for so many years, brought the Blessed Sacrament and together they celebrated the Rite of Viaticum, the administration of Communion with special prayers for the dying. The Latin word "*via*" means "the road" or the "way." Viaticum, then, is food for the journey along the way. One of the prayers in the rite explains clearly, "When the hour comes for us to pass from this life and join him, he strengthens us with this food for our journey and comforts us by this pledge of our resurrection."[14] The men knew that Frank was going against doctor's orders; they knew that he might not make it to San Diego. "[Viaticum] is the completion and crown of the Christian life on this earth, signifying that the Christian follows the Lord to eternal glory and the banquet of the heavenly kingdom."[15] They wouldn't meet again until the heavenly banquet.

Scripture recounts the story of men who carried a paralytic on a stretcher to Jesus. Because of the crowds, they couldn't get him through the door of the house so they lowered him through the roof to place him before Jesus (Lk 5:17-25). The St. Jude's men's group, through their faith, similarly enabled Frank, though crippled, to encounter the healing touch of Jesus. Like the paralytic, Frank, would also rise, pick up his stretcher and go home. Yet, his home would be the place that Jesus has prepared for him. For Jesus promised us, "I will come back again and take you to myself, so that where I am you also may be" (Jn 14:3).

When Ellyn went to visit dad at Special Care Hospital she walked in on the "California Wake." She had heard they had planned the visit but didn't know when. She was surprised to find laughing and storytelling, not tears and sad faces. But she was the one that felt a flood of tears coming on, so she quickly excused herself to the hallway for a quiet bawl.

As the men took leave of Frank, there were no tears. Guarding their emotions, with utmost trust in the Lord, they warmly shook hands and smiled. In the hallway, on his way out, Ed pulled Ellyn aside and quietly said, "We are all going to miss your dad. Take good care of him."

St. Brendan, a legendary fifth-century Irish monk, sailed away when he was thought to be eighty years old. Why did he leave Ireland? He set sail in a leather covered wooden vessel, not to escape famine or pestilence but in search of an isle called the Land of the Saints, in the shadows of the portals of Paradise.[16] He and a small band of monks ventured forth with faith as their guide and God as their traveling companion. During difficult moments in their journey St. Brendan comforted his fellow travelers with these words: "Brothers don't be scared, for God himself is aboard this boat."[17] Frank, like St. Brendan, at eighty-two years of age travelled with faith as his guide, and having received Viaticum, God was also aboard his boat.

The Healing of a Paralytic

One day as Jesus was teaching,
. . . some men brought on a stretcher
a man who was paralyzed;
they were trying to bring him in
and set [him] in his presence.
But not finding a way to bring him in
because of the crowd,
they went up on the roof and lowered him
on the stretcher through the tiles
into the middle in front of Jesus. . . .
he said to the man who was paralyzed,
"I say to you, rise, pick up your stretcher, and go home."
He stood up immediately before them,
picked up what he had been lying on,
and went home, glorifying God.

(Lk 5:18,19,24,25)

Chapter 22

The Town I Loved So Well

The Town I Loved So Well

In my memory I will always see
The town that I have loved so well
Where our school played ball by the gas yard wall
And we laughed through the smoke and the smell
Going home in the rain, running up the dark lane
Past the gaol, [jail] and down behind the fountain,
Those were happy days in so many, many ways
In the town I loved so well.

There was music there in the Derry air,
Like a language that we all could understand
I remember the day when I earned my first pay
When I played in a small pick-up band
There I spent my youth, and to tell you the truth
I was sad to leave it all behind me
For I learned about life and I found a wife
In the town I loved so well.

Phil Coulter

It took coordinated bicoastal teamwork to mobilize Frank's journey to California. Peter and I, on the West Coast, had the job to prepare our home and our hearts for dad's arrival. Our first task was to ensure that Frank had the necessary health care professionals. Who could be his primary care physician? It would be impossible to replace Dr. D. with his daily check-in carefully monitoring Frank's situation, constantly tweaking medications to keep his delicate condition in balance. But I remembered seeing an advertisement in our church bulletin for Dr. N., a mobile doctor in our parish who made house calls. We had known him and his family for many years as friends and parishioners, but not professionally. I thought I should call him to see if it would work.

"Dr. N., my dad is moving into our home from Pennsylvania. He's very sick. Would you be willing to take him on as a patient?"

"Of course. I'd be glad to. That's what I do!"

Well, that was a relief. The doctor coming to the house to see Frank would solve a lot of problems. He wouldn't need a wheelchair van to get out to appointments, which was good because there were days when he just wasn't up to it.

Next, I needed to think about professional nursing assistance, so I started interviewing companies that staffed home health aides. I learned that Frank would need a certified nursing assistant, a CNA, to help with his ADLs. Frank's size necessitated a well-trained professional not only for safety reasons but also to honor his concerns for privacy. Frank was very modest so I knew he would be uncomfortable with family members attending to his personal hygiene.

We also needed either a registered nurse, an RN, or a licensed vocational nurse, an LVN. RNs have more education and can administer medications and treatments, and also develop care plans in concert with the physicians. For home care, an LVN, couldn't administer medications or treatments but could offer comfort level care, monitor a patient's status, and provide communication between the patient, the family, and the physician.

Certainly, the cost of all this weighed significantly on our decision process. Fortunately, since Frank had been an insurance agent for forty years, we were sure that he was well covered, but this world was all new to us. We decided to start with twenty-four-hour CNA care and a twelve-hour shift, 8:00 a.m. to 8:00 p.m. for an LVN. Dr. N. could make a house call every couple of weeks and be on call as needed. That seemed to take care of the professional staffing we needed; now to prepare the house and the equipment Frank would need.

Ellyn had given me a long list of medical items to have ready in the house: a hospital bed, Hoyer lift, oxygen concentrator, shower chair, bedside commode, disposable diapers, diabetes test kit, blood pressure cuff, and a thermometer. I had never heard of some of these things before, but they would soon become part of our daily routine.

After I acquired the equipment, Peter asked how he could help set it up for Frank. We walked into the downstairs guest room, and I described how I wanted the room situated when suddenly Peter stopped me.

"Wait a minute. Frank's wheelchair won't fit through the doorway into the guest room."

"What?"

"Remember, his wheelchair is extra-wide. It won't clear the doorway."

We just stood there for a second, looking at each other blankly, holding back expletives, when I finally blurted out, "Where else can he go?"

Peter calmly responded, "I think the dining room is the place."

I nodded and said, "OK, let's take a look."

Our dining room had a wide entryway from the living room on one end, and a double door exit to the backyard on the other. Conveniently, a small pantry situated between the dining room and the kitchen could serve as a nurse's station for Frank's meds, clothes, and documents. Peter looked it over and said, "I think the dining room works. I can put the furniture in the garage and hang up curtains in the doorways for his privacy."

Peter then walked the entire ground floor of our home and the outside perimeter to identify where wheelchair access would be a problem. He concluded, "We are actually in pretty good shape. Our house surprisingly accommodates an extra-wide wheelchair. If Frank came in from the driveway to the back yard, and then in the back slider, the only modifications needed are a ramp from the driveway to the back patio and a small ramp over the slider."

"That's pretty good. Can you make the ramps?"

Peter nodded, "Oh, yeah. That's easy."

Relieved, I said, "Amazing. But what do we do about a shower?"

Peter scratched his head, "Yeah, I've been wondering about that. What do you think about installing a hand-held shower head with an extra-long hose into the outdoor faucet? There's hot water there and I can hang up a circular shower curtain around it."

"Well, it's a good thing we don't have Pennsylvania weather to worry about. It's not exactly five-star accommodations, but I think it'll work."

Meanwhile, on the East Coast, Ellyn and her husband Andy, were mobilizing the efforts to prepare for the launch. They returned to Mountain Top with their own long checklist. They went on a scavenger hunt, gathering the various odds and ends Frank wanted from the house. Dr. D. came up with a discharge plan that included over twenty prescriptions to get filled. It was all old school, nothing phoned in, just handwritten doctor scrawl on slips of paper that somehow pharmacists are trained to read. These were the meds that he had been tweaking daily to keep Frank's delicate condition in balance. No pressure. Then there was still the room at Little Flower that needed to be cleaned out.

At the last minute, Frank decided that he had to bring his lift-chair to California. This special chair had electronic controls that could lift him upright and forward into a standing position without requiring him to use his legs or arms. Of course, this chair was giant-sized extra-wide and extra-deep to accommodate Frank. At this point, Ellyn's blood pressure was going through the roof. It was not easy, physically, or emotionally, to coordinate the assembly of a mobile hospital unit to transport Frank safely to California. Ellyn wasn't sure she could take on the lift-chair project. She told him, "We're running out of time. I am still sorting out the medications, I'm not sure I can get to the chair. And Andy is still cleaning out your room in Little Flower. It has to be finished today."

Frank replied, "That's fine. I'll get Costigan to do it." So he called one of his men's lunch group buds. "Costigan, can you do me a favor?"

Costigan cheerfully replied, "For you, Frank, anything!"

"Can you disassemble my lift-chair so I can bring it to California?"

"Ah, Frank. I thought you were going to ask for something difficult! Sure, that's not a problem."

Without delay, Jack and his son Mark came over to the house to sort out the chair. Jack himself was aging, and not moving around as well as he once could. Yet, there he was, on his hands and knees, unscrewing bolts and unplugging wires to break it down into movable parts and carry it out to the driveway. Needless to say, Mark was crucial to the success of the operation. But who knew that this last-minute labor of love would provide a healing chair not only for Frank, but for family and friends in years to come?

Since Dr. D. was still trying to talk us out of the move, we continued to question the sanity of it. We could only remind ourselves that Frank had made the decision; he knew the situation and was willing to take the risk. And in his words, as he always liked to remind us, he's a tough old Irish bastard.

Then, suddenly, the day before the move, Ellyn noticed blood in Frank's catheter.

"Dad, this is a problem we have to take care of."

Frank sheepishly replied, "I didn't want to tell anyone for fear that they'd make me cancel the trip."

Ellyn reassured him, "Don't worry, Dad. This is just an adjustment not a deal-breaker. But we need to address it now."

Without fanfare, the day and the hour finally arrived. Like unsung heroes to the rescue, the McDonald twins arrived in the medical coach and backed it into the Mountain Top driveway. They methodically loaded the coach with the precious odds and ends on Frank's list until they got to the chair. With a quizzical look on his face, one of the twins asked, "Is this going too?"

The coach was already full, so it wasn't clear where the giant chair parts would go. But without a complaint or hesitation, the chair was quickly brought on board to the only open space left. It took over one side of the small bed where the "sleeping brother" would rest while the other brother drove. All packed up, the coach headed down to Special Care Hospital to pick up Frank.

The "California Wake" came to a climax with an emotional sendoff in the hospital parking lot. Mari and Jim were there with balloons, big hugs, and good wishes. Kevin Foley brought treasures from the homeland: Yuengling beer, kielbasa, and bottles of Glen Summit spring water. All the Special Care staff came out to wish Frank well. They helped him get situated in the small patient bed in the coach, much too short for someone 6'6." Then one by one they climbed aboard for one last hug, smiling through their tears. Ellyn gave Andy a quick kiss, climbed aboard, and away they went. The onlookers rimmed the parking lot as the medical coach disappeared around the corner and ventured out across the country toward a distant shore. Frank made a leap of faith. Taking courage in the Lord, like St. Peter, he was able to step out across uncertain waters.

Peter Walked on the Water toward Jesus

Then he made the disciples get into the boat
and precede him to the other side,
while he dismissed the crowds.
After doing so, he went up on the mountain
by himself to pray.
When it was evening he was there alone.
Meanwhile the boat, already a few miles offshore,
was being tossed about by the waves,
for the wind was against it.
During the fourth watch of the night, he came
toward them, walking on the sea.
When the disciples saw him walking on the sea
they were terrified.
"It is a ghost," they said, and they cried out in fear.
At once [Jesus] spoke to them,
"Take courage, it is I; do not be afraid."
Peter said to him in reply,
"Lord, if it is you, command me
to come to you on the water."
He said, "Come."
Peter got out of the boat and began to walk
on the water toward Jesus.
But when he saw how [strong] the wind was
he became frightened;
and, beginning to sink, he cried out, "Lord, save me!"
Immediately Jesus stretched out his hand
and caught him, and said to him,
"O you of little faith, why did you doubt?"
After they got into the boat, the wind died down.
Those who were in the boat did him homage,
saying, "Truly, you are the Son of God."

(Mt 14:22-33)

Chapter 23

The Best Christmas Present Ever

The sixty-five-year-old McDonald twins navigated steadily through snow and sleet, mountains and plains, tenaciously traversing the country to bring Frank safely to San Diego. One twin drove while the other slept, stopping only for gas and food. As the time for each meal approached, the twins offered Ellyn and Frank two take-out restaurants to choose between, but they always picked Cracker Barrel, the chain that cooks up home-style meals to go. The comfort food was good medicine during this time of uncertainty. The McDonalds phoned in the order ahead to ensure a quick pickup and a speedy return to the road to maintain the promised schedule. They were on a forty-eight-hour mission to deliver Frank to the other side.

Jesus asked the apostles to travel to the other side of the lake by boat. As they ventured across, with Jesus sleeping in the stern, a terrific storm arose and wildly tossed them about. When the apostles woke Jesus and asked him to save them, he rebuked them for having such little faith, yet easily calmed the storm. With St. Brendan as my model, I had faith that Jesus was aboard the medical coach. I prayed that he would calm every storm they encountered as they traveled three thousand miles from one side of the continent to the other.

For the duration Frank was cramped into a small bed, but all through the journey Ellyn rubbed his back to soothe his muscles and to keep him calm. It was crucial to Frank's comfort and stability that Ellyn was by his side all through this uncertain crossing. She was glad to be there to give him his meds and monitor his vital signs in case something went wrong.

Just before hitting the Rockies, I got a text from Ellyn asking for prayers because Frank didn't have any insulin. Somehow, one of the twenty medications had fallen through the cracks, and she couldn't get hold of Dr. D. for another prescription. Certainly, this was a storm that we would need Jesus' help to get us through. I prayed harder and posted a prayer request on Facebook to all our family and friends. The responses poured in, assuring us that many were praying Frank all the way to our door.

In San Diego, Peter and I had finished converting our dining room into a hospital room, but there was still no time to rest. With the help of God, Frank would be arriving soon. The Advent wreath, centered on the kitchen table, counting down the weeks, reminded us that Christmas was only nine days away. We were determined to transform our home posthaste into a holiday wonderland to make a grand welcome for Frank.

We decorated in record time. A dazzling Christmas tree garnished with little white lights and treasured family ornaments sprang up in the living room. Fragrant green boughs and bright red ribbons adorned the blazing hearth and encircled the bannisters while carols hummed softly in the background. Peter lit up the outside of our home like a gingerbread house piped with white royal icing. Shimmering white lights traced the roof lines and framed all the windows. It was a beacon to welcome our weary travelers and to signal there was room at this inn. But most important of all, the crèche nestled under the tree retold the story of what this celebration is all about. The nativity scene had a modest stable to shelter the figurines of Mary, Joseph, the donkey, shepherds, sheep, and an ox. They gathered around an empty manger, waiting with great anticipation for arrival of the baby Jesus. In the fullness of time, on the darkest of days, he came into our midst, the light of the world, for our salvation.

Under the English Penal Laws of the sixteenth and seventeenth centuries, Irish Catholics were forbidden to practice their religion, including having a Christmas crèche. Celebrating the incarnation of our Lord gave such hope to the oppressed people that they risked imprisonment by carving stones into rough nativity figurines for their manger scenes. When the English would come to inspect their homes, the stones were scattered in the garden to go undetected as religious artifacts. Today, many Irish families retain the tradition of having a nativity scene. Some like to wait until Christmas Eve to place baby Jesus in the manger, and on the feast of the Epiphany add the three wise men and their camels, bearing gifts of gold, frankincense, and myrrh.

According to another Irish Christmas tradition, brightly burning candles are placed in the windows to signal that the Holy Family are welcome, unlike that first Christmas in Bethlehem. All the houses in our neighborhood had lights, so we tied red balloons to the mailbox to let the McDonald twins know they had found the right place, that there was room in our home for Frank.

Just as the house was finally ready, the doorbell rang. As we opened the door, we were greeted by our first CNA as he chanted, "I'm here!" From the very first moment we laid eyes on Reynaldo, we knew he was handpicked by God to care for Frank. A gentle soul with a small frame but a very large heart was ordained to take on this ministry. We quickly learned to look forward to the same chant, "I'm here!" that Reynaldo repeated every time he arrived at our door.

My heart fluttered as I read the text from Ellyn that they were ten minutes away. Peter, Reynaldo, and I went up our steep curved driveway to greet the medical coach. As they pulled up, I had to remind myself to breathe. He is here. Frank is here. He made it! He is alive!

The McDonald twins parked up at the street, telling us that backing down the steep driveway wouldn't be safe. It was a sight to behold as they helped Frank out of the coach and into his wheelchair on our street. I thought my heart would beat right out of my chest. Frank, though pale and weak, was so happy and so relieved to be here.

Though he had come three thousand miles, the most dangerous leg of the trip still lay ahead. It took Peter and both McDonald twins to wrestle the heavily weighted wheelchair down our steep winding driveway and into the house. The prized Christmas package had finally been delivered, safe and sound. Jesus had certainly been in the coach calming every storm.

The Calming of a Storm at Sea

[Jesus] said to them,
"Let us cross to the other side of the lake."
So they set sail, and while they were sailing
he fell asleep.
A squall blew over the lake, and they were
taking in water and were in danger.
They came and woke him saying,
"Master, master, we are perishing!"
He awakened, rebuked the wind and the waves,
and they subsided and there was a calm.
Then he asked them, "Where is your faith?"
But they were filled with awe and amazed
and said to one another,
"Who then is this, who commands
even the winds and the sea,
and they obey him?"

(Lk 8: 22-25)

Chapter 24

Christmas Day

St. Andrew Christmas Novena

Hail and blessed be the hour and moment
in which the Son of God was born
of the most pure Virgin Mary,
at midnight, in Bethlehem, in piercing cold.
In that hour vouchsafe, I beseech thee,
O my God, to hear my prayer and grant my desires
through the merits of our Savior Jesus Christ,
and of his blessed Mother.
Amen.

At 5:00 a.m. I awoke with a jolt, praising God for the miracle that my father was safely here in our home, in San Diego, on Christmas morning. Ever since my sisters and I were young girls, Frank would remind us, "Don't forget to say the Christmas Novena!" It was to be prayed fifteen times a day from the Feast of St. Andrew, November 30, until Christmas Eve to request a special intention. Over these past weeks, I hadn't managed to say it fifteen times and some days, not even once, but surely my prayer was answered. Frank was here. On this most glorious day, celebrating the incarnation of our Lord and Savior, Jesus Christ, my husband, our three children, Reynaldo, and Frank were all under the same roof

My thoughts turned to the journey of the Holy Family, with Mary in advanced pregnancy riding on a donkey, all the way from Nazareth to Bethlehem. It would have taken longer than forty-eight hours and there was no Cracker Barrel along the way. Upon arrival, they found no room at the inn, and no family to welcome them. I was abundantly grateful that we were able to provide room for Frank. In many ways, the medical coach was the donkey, the dining room was the stable, and the hospital bed was the manger. We had received Christ into our home in the face of the sick, the invalid, the homeless, and the hungry.

I showered, put on my Christmas dress, and crept down the stairs to wish Frank a very Merry Christmas! His eyes twinkled and his smile said everything. He was so happy to be here with us. I had planned to make a special breakfast and then go to Mass with my family, until Reynaldo pulled me aside.

"Noreen, we are out of disposable briefs."

My jaw dropped as I looked blankly at Reynaldo and replied, "OK. Extra-large, disposable briefs?"

Reynaldo nodded his head.

Well, I wasn't going to Mass that morning after all. Instead, I was on a mission to find a store that sold extra-large disposable briefs and was open on Christmas. I drove to the nearest pharmacy, but it wasn't open. I drove to the next one and, thanks be to God, it was open, and they had disposable briefs, but unfortunately, they were out of extra-large. As is often the case, the third time's a charm, and the next pharmacy was open and had the right size in stock. Disaster averted. I returned home with the prized package to save the day!

That little adventure set the tone for the remainder of the day. We lowered our expectations and learned to live in the moment and be grateful for the small things. We had a low-key day, opening presents, playing games, nibbling on treats, and cooking Christmas dinner.

Since the dining room had become Frank's bedroom, we set up the dinner table in the living room. Frank pulled up to the head of the table in his wheelchair, Peter at the foot, and the rest of us, including our aides, filled in around the sides. Before we started the meal, I led the Christmas blessing, which was an emotional moment. My Nana had always said the special blessing that my mother took over after Nana died. Now this was the first Christmas without my mother, and the prayer had fallen to me. It was painful and comforting all at the same time.

May all the days of all the years
That God has still in store
Be filled with every joy and grace
To bless you more and more;
May hope of heart and peace of mind
Beside you ever stay, and that's the special prayer I have
For you this Christmas Day!

Dinner consisted of our traditional turkey, mashed potatoes, gravy, broccoli casserole, cranberry sauce, stuffing, sweet potatoes, and Christmas cookies for dessert. Every morsel was much needed comfort food and a step above Cracker Barrel.

Emotionally and physically worn from the day, we were all eager to go to bed early. The dishes were done and Frank all settled in when I went to check his blood sugar and say our nighttime prayers. Though this was still fairly new to me, I had grown accustomed to the process. I was in charge of the morning and bedtime tests while the LVN took the lunch and dinner tests. I had to prick one of Frank's sore fingers for a drop of blood and then read the meter for his blood glucose level. I was accustomed to seeing around 100mg/dL in the morning and as high as 150mg/dL before bed. But tonight, I nearly fainted when I saw his bedtime blood sugar level was over 400 mg/dL.

I didn't let on to Frank that it was ridiculously high, I just went out to the kitchen to call Dr. N.

"Dr. N., Merry Christmas. I'm sorry to bother you but Frank's blood sugar is over 400. What should I do?"

"It's going to be OK. I'm sure it's just because of all the Christmas food. Does Frank seem to be in any distress?"

"No. He actually seems quite content after the day of celebration."

"All right, Noreen, just give him the appropriate dose of insulin on the sliding scale. Wait two hours and then retest. If it hasn't gone below 300mg/dL, then go to the emergency room. I am fairly certain it will have resolved by then."

"Dr. N., thank you so much for taking my call and talking me through this. I really appreciate it. I hope you enjoy the rest of your Christmas. Wish your family a Merry Christmas for me."

What had I done? Have I harmed Frank? I had to stay strong and carry on. What does dad say? Keep at it, Riley! I administered the dose of insulin, and we said our prayers. I didn't need to worry dad that if things didn't turn around, we may have a hospital visit. I kept my prayers for a quick recovery in the silence of my fast-beating heart. I turned on the TV and just tried to relax with dad for a couple of hours.

Thanks be to God, when I took the second blood sugar test, it had gone down. We were in the clear! As I fell into bed, I thanked God for this day, for my family, for the disposable briefs, for the blood sugar levels heading in the right direction. I turned on the baby monitor next to my bed to listen in on Frank for any signs of distress throughout the night and fell right to sleep, knowing that God is with us.

God Is with Us

The angel of the Lord appeared to [Joseph] in a dream and said,
"Joseph, son of David,
do not be afraid to take Mary your wife into your home.
For it is through the Holy Spirit
that this child has been conceived in her.
She will bear a son and you are to name him Jesus,
because he will save his people from their sins."
All this took place to fulfill
what the Lord had said through the prophet:
Behold, the virgin shall conceive and bear a son,
and they shall name him Emmanuel,
which means "God is with us."

(Mt 1:20-23)

Chapter 25

I Am

> "But," said Moses to God,
> "if I go to the Israelites and say to them,
> 'The God of your ancestors has sent me to you,'
> and they ask me,
> 'What is his name?' what do I tell them?"
> God replied to Moses:
> I am who I am.
> Then he added: This is what you will tell the Israelites:
> I AM has sent me to you.
> God spoke further to Moses:
> This is what you will say to the Israelites:
> The LORD, the God of your ancestors,
> the God of Abraham, the God of Isaac,
> and the God of Jacob, has sent me to you.
> This is my name forever;
> this is my title for all generations.
>
> (Ex 3:13-15)

The euphoria of having Frank with us quickly gave way to the anxiety of our newfound responsibility for caring for him with his delicate state of health. After Ellyn departed for Sacramento, I was left to sort out the long list of medications. Some were to be taken every three hours, some every six hours, some with food, some without food, and some without calcium products. I wanted to cry. What had I done? I didn't know what I was doing. I didn't want to cause any harm to Frank. I was in over my head.

God, the hearer of my prayers, sent Sergio to rescue me. Sergio, our twelve-hour-a-day LVN, was always calm, extremely knowledgeable, and exact. Always. Whatever was a mystery to me, Sergio sorted out. He anticipated Frank's needs—and mine too. With his sly sense of humor, he cared for us and kept us at ease.

We eventually got into a routine. Each morning as my feet hit the floor, my constant and fervent prayer was, "God, guide my feet, guide my hands, guide my heart, and guard my words."

I would descend the stairs to the dining room to greet Frank with a cheery, "Good morning! How was your night?"

Inevitably Frank responded, "Pretty good."

After I got the coffee going, I tested Frank's blood sugar level, calculated the necessary dose of insulin, then gave him an injection. I had always been squeamish about medical procedures. Blood and needles could make me faint in seconds. So, it was shocking that I could administer medical care for my dad; it didn't bother me one bit. I was given all the grace I needed to carry it out. Next, I would start a nebulizer breathing treatment for his COPD, turn the news channel on the TV, and get breakfast ready. Right after the breathing treatment, I served Frank a bagel with cream cheese and jelly, a large cup of coffee in a Notre Dame mug and handed him his newspaper.

In those early morning hours Frank and I would have our best chats. He would tell me all kinds of treasured stories. He told me about the homing pigeons that he kept as a boy. He raised generations of them from chicks. His father, Jack, would drive the birds out to the farmlands where he sold insurance, as far as twenty miles away, and then release them. Remarkably, the birds always made their way home. Then Frank told me about his dog Trixie. When the family went on vacation, they left his "best buddy" in

Scranton with his aunt. A week later, when they arrived back home in the middle of the night, there was Trixie, sitting in the middle of the road in front of the house, waiting for Frank. And Scranton was twenty miles away! I noticed the running theme here—against all odds, his pets were always able to return home. I wondered if Frank was having similar thoughts of returning home to Pennsylvania.

I loved his stories about the past generations of women in my family that worked or volunteered for the Church. Aunt Mary was the housekeeper for the rectory. She shopped, cooked, and cleaned for three resident priests. Aunt Grace washed and ironed the altar linens. Nana, famous for her jokes, was the master of ceremonies for St. John's altar society. There was only one professed religious in the family that he knew of, Sister Defrosa, yet everyone was religious. We were raised Irish Catholic and remained practicing Catholics throughout our lives.

Frank was very conscious of the news, particularly the weather since it determined his daily activities. He loved his shower; it was like a trip to the spa. Since it had to be outside, it depended on the weather—not too windy, not too cold, just right. He would either joyfully declare it "a good shower day" or sadly "a bad shower day." Right about that time each day, Sergio would arrive for his twelve-hour shift and work with Reynaldo to care for Frank's hygienic needs with or without the shower.

Without fail, the morning mail would bring a couple of letters or cards from Frank's people back in Mountain Top. And like clockwork, once a week his high school buddy, Billy Dugan, would send a newspaper article reviewing the Notre Dame football season and the latest scoop on number five, Manti Te'o. And of course, the phone rang several times a day for Frank, from friends and relatives around the country. We had to adjust to living with a celebrity.

After lunch there would always be a nap and then a "walk." Sergio and Reynaldo would take Frank out in his wheelchair with the dogs to wander through the neighborhood. On Frank's good days he wanted to push the limit and go down the big hill. Easy for him to say. I don't know which was harder, going down the hill without letting it roll out of control or pushing the 350-pound wheelchair up the hill without it rolling down backwards over whoever was behind it. Though Frank called Reynaldo "mighty mouse," neither Sergio nor Reynaldo were big guys. I had visions of newspaper headlines flashing before my eyes:

"Death by wheelchair."

"Double fatality. Invalid runs over aides."

"Walk in neighborhood gone bad."

"Pancaked by a wheelchair."

But on the daily walks Frank got to know all the neighbors. One day, Frank informed me that Lois across the street was celebrating her ninetieth birthday.

"Noreen, can you buy a box of candy for Lois and pick up a birthday cake? Let's invite her and her daughter over for a little party!"

Lois had been living with her daughter for five years and, honestly, the little social outing was good for all of us.

My next-door neighbor stopped me on the street to ask how Frank was doing. She told me that when she brought her kids home from school they would often stop and chat with Frank while he was out on a "walk." After one of those visits, her youngest daughter endearingly asked, "Mom, how come we like Frank so much?"

After an afternoon nap, at the end of the day everyone in the house would have dinner together. Some evenings Frank would feel too weak to get out of bed, so we would wheel his hospital bed into the family room to join everyone for the evening meal. But before we began to eat, Frank always led us in the grace before meals.

Bless us, O Lord
and these thy gifts
which we are about to receive
from thy bounty
through Christ our Lord.
Amen.
May God provide for the wants of others
and may the souls of the faithful departed
through the mercy of God rest in peace,
Amen.

This is the prayer Frank's parents, Jack and Anna always said, adding the line to lift up those in need and those that have gone before us in faith. It was particularly comforting now that mom had joined the faithful departed.

Monday's dinner was special. At Sergio's instigation we started celebrating Mexican Mondays. It included what Sergio liked to call "the Mexicanization of Frank": slick back his hair, put on Mexican music, and eat Mexican food. The best Mondays were when Sergio would make his world-renowned Mexican shrimp cocktail. When I made the dinner, I would inevitably apologize for making it too spicy, look around the table and find them all laughing.

"Noreen, this isn't spicy at all. Pass the hot sauce."

I would just roll my eyes and respond, "OK, fine."

After dinner Reynaldo and Sergio would get Frank ready for bed and then it would be time for Sergio to go home for the evening. Sergio never left without giving me a detailed account of the day, asking if I had any questions, and reminding me to text him if I needed anything during the night. We were so blessed to have Sergio.

Frank would like to relax with a little evening TV until it was time for his nighttime blood sugar check, prayers, and bed. The bedtime prayers were one of my favorite parts of the day. Reynaldo was a devout Catholic and would eagerly join in. We would break out the hymnals and sing four or five favorites. Reynaldo's beautiful voice could sing out "On Eagle's Wings" like no other. Then we would say one Our Father, a Hail Mary, and a Glory Be, followed by spontaneous prayers for whatever was on our hearts. But night after night, Frank had the very same petitions:

"I pray for: Pope Francis, all those I left behind in Mountain Top, especially Mari, and all those poor buggers who are still in the hospital, back where I was. For my son-in-law, Peter, that he will turn Catholic. . ."

And shaking his finger at the heavens, he'd add ". . . And you'd better hurry it up, Lord, because I want to see it in my lifetime, and I am running out of time."

Peter and I had met in physics class when we were sophomores at the Catholic University of America. After we were engaged, my father said, "I like Peter. He's a good man. But really, how did you manage to get engaged to the only non-Catholic at the Catholic University of America?"

After thirty years of fervent prayer for Peter to become Catholic, Frank had resorted to storming the gates of heaven for his prayer to be answered, right now. Nonetheless, the prayer time always left us feeling good about the day. We left all our cares in God's hands.

Frank's health was up and down. There were good days and bad days. On the bad days, I would start to prepare myself that this may be when the angels come for Frank. But without fail, the next day he would bounce back and regain his strength. I had a hard time switching gears from "he's going to die" to "he's going to live." It was difficult for me to rebound from mourning at the prospect of losing him to being his advocate for continuing the good fight to keep him alive. I found myself wanting to know how long he had to live. Then I remembered the "I AM" poem that my mother often quoted:

I AM

I was regretting the past and fearing the future.
Suddenly, my Lord was speaking:
"My name is I AM."
He paused. I waited. He continued,
When you live in the past with its mistakes and regrets, it is hard.
I am not there.
My name is not I WAS.
When you live in the future, with its problems and fears, it is hard.
I am not there.
My name is not I WILL BE.
When you live in this moment, it is not hard. I am here.
My name is I AM.

Helen Mallicoat

Chapter 26

Give Me A Chance

D r. N. arrived at our home with his staff for Frank's mobile checkup. As with all the medical professionals that interacted with Frank, they started the examination with the usual drill: "What is your name? What is the date? What is your date of birth? Who is the president?"

Frank usually behaved himself until they got to the "president" question. With a straight face he would playfully answer "Roosevelt," or "Kennedy," or "Bush," but never the correct answer, Obama. You could see the doctor's eyebrows raise until I said, "Dad! Stop that! They want to know if you are with it or not!" Everyone laughed, but we all knew that in his condition it was remarkable that he was sharp! Even sharp enough to make a joke like that!

After a thorough evaluation Dr. N. adjusted his medications and ordered certain in-home treatments: physical therapy, chest X-rays, dental care, podiatrist. Then, Dr. N. took me aside to break it to me gently that Frank was seriously ill.

"Noreen, I am so sorry to tell you that your father is a very sick man. He has several very serious medical conditions affecting his heart and his lungs, and he also has diabetes. Any one of these could contribute to his demise at any time. He has COPD, CHF, and atrial fibrillation just for starters."

Nodding my head, I slowly responded, "Yes, Dr. N. I know. I know his condition is very serious. I really appreciate you taking him on as a patient."

"Does your father have an advanced directive, or a living will? An advanced directive provides instructions for a situation in the future when a patient is unable to make decisions. A living will is a specific type of advanced directive that takes effect when a patient is terminally ill, or unable to speak for themselves. It is important to know what your father's wishes are for his health care treatment instructions in the event of end-stage medical condition or permanent unconsciousness."

I carefully worded my reply, "Frank has a living will. He clearly describes his goals in this way: 'If I have an end stage medical condition or other extreme irreversible medical condition, my goals in making medical decisions are as follows: "Give me a chance."' He wants all life-prolonging procedures to be used as necessary, including CPR, a ventilator, and kidney dialysis. He is not ready to die. Frank wants to live."

Dr. N. nodded his head. "OK, that's really great. I think it would be beneficial then to also fill out a POLST (Physician Orders for Life-Sustaining Treatment)[18] form. It would be good to have this conversation with your dad at this point. I will leave this form for you to discuss with him and we can review when I return. In the meantime, let me know if you have any questions."

Looking over the POLST, I noticed that it was a California form, so he wouldn't have seen this in Pennsylvania. It seemed self-explanatory. It includes a checklist of questions.

HIPAA PERMITS DISCLOSURE OF POLST TO OTHER HEALTH CARE PROVIDERS AS NECESSARY		

Physician Orders for Life-Sustaining Treatment (POLST)

First follow these orders, then contact **Physician/NP/PA.** A copy of the signed POLST form is a legally valid physician order. Any section not completed implies full treatment for that section. POLST complements an Advance Directive and is not intended to replace that document.

EMSA #111 B (Effective 4/1/2017)*

Patient Last Name:	Date Form Prepared:
Patient First Name:	Patient Date of Birth:
Patient Middle Name:	Medical Record #: *(optional)*

A
Check One

CARDIOPULMONARY RESUSCITATION (CPR): *If patient has no pulse and is not breathing.*
If patient is NOT in cardiopulmonary arrest, follow orders in Sections B and C.

☐ Attempt Resuscitation/CPR (Selecting CPR in Section A **requires** selecting Full Treatment in Section B)

☐ Do Not Attempt Resuscitation/DNR (Allow Natural Death)

B
Check One

MEDICAL INTERVENTIONS: *If patient is found with a pulse and/or is breathing.*

☐ **Full Treatment** – primary goal of prolonging life by all medically effective means.
In addition to treatment described in Selective Treatment and Comfort-Focused Treatment, use intubation, advanced airway interventions, mechanical ventilation, and cardioversion as indicated.
☐ *Trial Period of Full Treatment.*

☐ **Selective Treatment** – goal of treating medical conditions while avoiding burdensome measures.
In addition to treatment described in Comfort-Focused Treatment, use medical treatment, IV antibiotics, and IV fluids as indicated. Do not intubate. May use non-invasive positive airway pressure. Generally avoid intensive care.
☐ *Request transfer to hospital only if comfort needs cannot be met in current location.*

☐ **Comfort-Focused Treatment** – primary goal of maximizing comfort.
Relieve pain and suffering with medication by any route as needed; use oxygen, suctioning, and manual treatment of airway obstruction. Do not use treatments listed in Full and Selective Treatment unless consistent with comfort goal. *Request transfer to hospital only if comfort needs cannot be met in current location.*

Additional Orders: _____

C
Check One

ARTIFICIALLY ADMINISTERED NUTRITION: *Offer food by mouth if feasible and desired.*

☐ Long-term artificial nutrition, including feeding tubes. Additional Orders: _____
☐ Trial period of artificial nutrition, including feeding tubes. _____
☐ No artificial means of nutrition, including feeding tubes. _____

D

INFORMATION AND SIGNATURES:

Discussed with: ☐ Patient (Patient Has Capacity) ☐ Legally Recognized Decisionmaker

☐ Advance Directive dated _____, available and reviewed → Health Care Agent if named in Advance Directive:
☐ Advance Directive not available Name: _____
☐ No Advance Directive Phone: _____

Signature of Physician / Nurse Practitioner / Physician Assistant (Physician/NP/PA)
My signature below indicates to the best of my knowledge that these orders are consistent with the patient's medical condition and preferences.

Print Physician/NP/PA Name:	Physician/NP/PA Phone #:	Physician/PA License #, NP Cert. #:
Physician/NP/PA Signature: *(required)*		Date:

Signature of Patient or Legally Recognized Decisionmaker
I am aware that this form is voluntary. By signing this form, the legally recognized decisionmaker acknowledges that this request regarding resuscitative measures is consistent with the known desires of, and with the best interest of, the individual who is the subject of the form.

Print Name:	Relationship: *(write self if patient)*
Signature: *(required)*	Date:	Your POLST may be added to a secure electronic registry to be accessible by health providers, as permitted by HIPAA.
Mailing Address (street/city/state/zip):	Phone Number:	

SEND FORM WITH PATIENT WHENEVER TRANSFERRED OR DISCHARGED

Even before I shared the POLST with Frank, I could easily interpret his directive to "Give me a chance" to the obvious choices: Attempt Resuscitation/CPR, Full Treatment, and Long-term artificial nutrition by tube. I waited until our breakfast chat the next morning to discuss it with him.

As he was finishing his second mug of coffee, I showed Frank the POLST. He read it, looked me directly in the eye, and reiterated, "Give me a chance!"

I smiled and said, "Of course Dad, that's my job! Have no fear." I was meeting him where he was at.

I would have made different choices, but it wasn't my call. It was entirely Frank's. My responsibility was solely to support his wishes. Selfishly, I would have preferred that Frank remain in our home with comfort care and die peacefully without what could be violent medical interventions to prolong his life. What would be the outcome if Frank was resuscitated? Would that be painful for him? Does it make sense at this point? Does he really understand what that means when he says, "Give me a chance"? It could include CPR, shocking his heart, putting a tube down his throat, attaching him to a ventilator to help him breathe. Would he need to be tied down to keep all the tubes in place? Would he really want to spend the remainder of his days on a ventilator? According to experts from the American Thoracic Society, "A ventilator can be lifesaving, but its use has risks. It doesn't fix the problem that led to the person needing the ventilator in the first place; it just helps support a person until other treatments become effective, or the person gets better on their own. . . . Some people never improve enough to be taken off the ventilator."[19]

When a patient is placed on a ventilator, an endotracheal tube (ET) is inserted through the mouth or nose and passed between the vocal cords into the windpipe. The ET prevents a patient from talking or eating by mouth. Is this really the way he wants to die, living out his last days on a ventilator?

Alternatively, if Frank didn't have a POLST or had chosen to receive a trial period of full treatment and subsequently needed to be placed on a ventilator, my sisters and I would have a weighty decision to make. Catholic teaching indicates that "life-sustaining treatment certainly can be removed while maintaining respect for the equal dignity of human beings. First, though it might be foreseen that death is likely, it cannot be intended that death come about (either by an action or omission). Second, it must be reasonably determined that the burden of the medical treatment is disproportionate with respect to any expected benefit. . . . The ventilator could be withdrawn precisely as part of what is necessary to respect [Frank's] equal dignity and worth as a human being."[20] Consequently, we either could keep him on the ventilator indefinitely or determine when to take him off. This decision can be devastating and divisive for families. I prayed that we would not be faced with this ethical dilemma.

You Know Neither the Day nor the Hour

"Then the kingdom of heaven will be like ten virgins
who took their lamps and went out to meet
the bridegroom.
Five of them were foolish and five were wise.
The foolish ones said to the wise,
'Give us some of your oil, for our lamps are going out.'
But the wise ones replied,
'No, for there may not be enough for us and you.
Go instead to the merchants and buy some
for yourselves.'
While they went off to buy it,
the bridegroom came and those who were ready
went into the wedding feast with him.
Then the door was locked.
Afterwards the other virgins came and said,
'Lord, Lord, open the door for us!'
But he said in reply, 'Amen, I say to you,
I do not know you.'
Therefore, stay awake,
for you know neither the day nor the hour."

(Mt 25:1-2, 8-13)

Chapter 27

The Body of Christ

Christ has no body on earth now but yours,
no hands but yours, no feet but yours;
yours are the eyes through which
he looks with compassion on the world;
yours are the feet with which he walks to do good;
yours are the hands with which he blesses all the world.

St. Teresa of Ávila

The scriptures are filled with accounts of Jesus ministering to the sick and the marginalized. Through the healing touch of Jesus, the lame walked, the blind saw, the deaf heard, lepers were cleansed, and the dead were raised (Mt 11:5). A hemorrhaging woman's faith boldly drew her to Jesus and touching the hem of his garment cured her of the affliction that she had suffered for twelve years (Mk 5:25-29). A faith-filled man named Jairus invited Jesus into his home to heal his dying daughter. Jesus "took the child by the hand and said to her, 'Talitha koum,' which means, 'Little girl, I say to you, arise!'" (Mk 5:41). And she did! I longed to bring the healing touch of Jesus into our home for my father. I prayed that I could bring the hem of Jesus' garment to him. I wanted my father to arise.

On Sunday, like Jairus, I could bring Jesus to my home. The Catholic Church continues the ministry of Christ to the sick and homebound today through Pastoral Care of the Sick (PCS).[21] PCS provides a rite for Communion of the Sick that can be celebrated by clergy as well as lay ministers. As an extraordinary minister of Holy Communion, with the permission of my pastor, I could bring the Blessed Sacrament, the Real Presence of Christ, from Mass to my homebound father.

On Sundays, the Lord's Day, I eagerly went to Mass, for the Eucharist is the source and summit of the Christian life. It was so comforting to join my parish community to praise and worship God, and to give thanks for my many blessings even in this difficult time. I felt the deep need to encounter the Real Presence of Christ not only in the Eucharist, but also in the priest, the Word, and the assembly filled with many friends and familiar faces.[22] The encounter with Christ at Sunday Mass filled me spiritually and sustained me as I faced challenges throughout the week.

The connection between the parish celebration of the Eucharist and ministry to the sick, particularly on the Lord's Day, was easy to see. The sick and those that care for them are remembered in the Prayers of the Faithful, yet more importantly, they receive the Body of Christ that sacramentally unites them to the Lord and also unites them with their parish community from which their illness has separated them. I joined other ministers who brought Holy Communion to the sick and homebound. Each of us carried a pyx, a circular metal locket, into which our pastor placed the Blessed Sacrament and sent us forth from the community out to our absent sisters and brothers, on mission, as all the baptized are called to be. The dismissal of the ministers from the liturgy profoundly witnessed to the congregation the parish's pastoral care for those whose illness prevented them from joining in person.

Arriving home directly from Mass, I invited everyone in the household—family, friends, and caregivers—to gather in the living room to celebrate the Rite of Communion of the Sick. The Church envisions this beautiful liturgy to be a joyful celebration that includes those that share in this ministry of comfort and care. We took turns proclaiming scripture readings and leading the prayers. We sang hymns that spoke of a pilgrim's journey toward God. Our musical family and friends would often add piano, guitar, and trumpet. We made the celebration of the rite special and joy-filled. The centerpiece, of course, was offering the Body of Christ to Frank, the food for his journey home to God. It was a precious moment. We became the men lowering the paralytic through the roof of the house to Jesus (Lk 5:17-26). Frank had indeed touched the hem of Jesus' garment.

We were tremendously blessed to minister to Frank, but the greater blessing was Frank's ministry to us. His faith in the Eucharist was a living testimony to the preaching of St. Augustine, "Believe what you see, see what you believe and become what you are: the Body of Christ." Here are just a few ways Frank ministered to us.

CHRIS

Chris was often a regular part of our Sunday gatherings. When I couldn't leave the house, Chris would bring Holy Communion to Frank. It was also like an extension of our choir days where Chris enthusiastically shared his faith, his beautiful voice, and his amazing trumpet playing. Frank had played the trumpet all through high school and college, so it was very special when Chris played Frank's trumpet.

One Sunday, the usually upbeat Chris seemed really down. Frank, sensing that something was wrong, asked, "Chris, what's up?"

Chris answered, "Ugh, I am pretty disgusted with my family right now."

Frank pressed him, "Why, what happened?"

Chris confessed, "My uncle found out that I am gay and is unaccepting of who I am."

We could see how painful this was for Chris. Without hesitating, from his hospital bed, Frank looked Chris straight in the eye and said, "Chris, if it's OK with you, I'd like to be your uncle."

Very moved by this spontaneous outpouring of acceptance, Chris and Frank shook hands in a very tender expression of their mutual respect and affection.

DAVE

It was a delight to have Joan and Dave McDonald come home with me after Mass. Joan, a dedicated choir member, could add the alto part to every hymn ever written and Dave would mightily proclaim the Gospel. There was a special connection between Dave and Frank. Dave had a special place in Frank's heart, maybe because they were both salesmen with a gift for connecting with people, but it was more likely the deep faith that they shared. Both were big, strong men with a quiet way of witnessing their faith without a lot of words but in everything they did in life.

One day, Dave sadly shared that he had lost his job. Softly and confidently, Frank responded that he would pray that Dave would find just the right job. No one was surprised, least of all, Frank, when only a couple of weeks later, Dave landed an even better job than the one he'd lost. Frank felt sure that Dave's new position was an answer to his prayers. From then on, whenever Dave walked in the door, Frank would greet him and ask him how his work was going, just to check on the continued success of his prayer request.

MURPHY

Back in November, before the move to California, Frank insisted that I get a puppy. He was worried that I would be heartbroken when my fourteen-year-old dog, Kona, died and thought a new puppy would ease the pain when the day came. Kona wasn't a service dog, an officially trained, "card-carrying" canine companion, yet she provided great emotional support for everyone in the family, but mostly for me. I also had a twelve-year-old golden retriever, Sophie, but Frank persisted, and every phone call included the interrogation, "Did you get that puppy yet?" So, I relented and found a litter of puppies that would be ready for pick-up in January.

One Sunday morning, the day finally arrived. But now we also had Frank! A big group of us planned to go pick out a puppy from the large litter of Labrador retrievers. I went to early Mass and brought the Blessed Sacrament home to celebrate the Rite for Communion of the Sick before going for the puppy. Chris was there, Mollie was home, and Greg was on his way over. As we got started, we were surprised to see Greg walk in with a young lady. Greg introduced her: "This is Christina." Nodding towards me, he said, "This is my mom. This is what she does."

That got a chuckle from everyone.

I greeted her warmly, "Hi Christina. Welcome."

As we celebrated the rite, complete with piano, trumpet, singing, and readings, Frank rested in his wheelchair next to me at the piano. Throughout the whole rite Christina sat alongside Greg on the couch, wide-eyed. I thought, well, she is either in or she's out. This could be a bit overwhelming for a newcomer to take in. She had been told she was coming along to pick out a puppy. Would this be the last time we'd see her?

After the rite we all left to pick out Murphy. From the litter we chose the one that purred when you petted him. Without question he would be a lot of fun yet added another level of craziness to our days that we really didn't need. But Frank enjoyed Murphy, and—thankfully—Christina stuck around.

Celebrating the Rite of Communion of the Sick continued to be a tremendous blessing to Frank and to us, although it was important to take Frank's health and stamina into consideration. The rite for Communion of the Sick in Ordinary Circumstances closely follows the pattern of Sunday Mass.[23] It includes Introductory Rites, a Penitential Rite, Liturgy of the Word, Liturgy of Holy Communion, and Concluding Rites. It may be necessary, however, to adapt and simplify the celebration. For those in a hospital or institution, there is a special abbreviated rite.[24]

Frank relished the music and the lively celebrations, yet some days he wasn't up to it. If he couldn't get out of bed, we wheeled him, hospital bed and all, into the living room next to the piano. Most often we used the readings of the day, but at times a shorter reading was all he could handle. Then there were days he needed to just stay quietly in his bedroom, and we would only pray an Our Father and give him Holy Communion. Afterwards, I played hymns on the piano softly, hoping the music soothed his suffering.

By this point Frank needed to be on oxygen, so any open flame was hazardous. That ruled out lighting the candle in the special crucifix candlestick that mom always used when Joe Baltz brought Holy Communion. I love my candles, but I loved my dad even more, so giving it up was easy.

These were difficult days, yet we trusted that we were in the hands of God and we prayed that we could see our troubles through the eyes of God.

Be Thou My Vision

Be Thou my Vision, O Lord of my heart;
Naught be all else to me, save that Thou art;
Thou my best Thought, by day or by night,
Waking or sleeping, Thy presence my light.

Be Thou my Wisdom, and Thou my true Word;
I ever with Thee and Thou with me, Lord;
Thou my great Father, I Thy true son;
Thou in me dwelling, and I with Thee one.

Be Thou my battle Shield, Sword for the fight;
Be Thou my Dignity, Thou my Delight;
Thou my soul's Shelter, Thou my high Tow'r:
Raise Thou me heav'nward, O Pow'r of my pow'r.

Riches I heed not, nor man's empty praise,
Thou mine Inheritance, now and always:
Thou and Thou only, first in my heart,
High King of Heaven, my Treasure Thou art.

High King of Heaven, my victory won,
May I reach Heaven's joys, O bright Heav'n's Sun!
Heart of my own heart, whatever befall,
Still be my Vision, O Ruler of all.

Dallán Forgaill

Chapter 28

The Claddagh:
Love, Loyalty, and Friendship

After my mother's death, with a heavy heart, I poked through her drawers and belongings. My eyes lit up, though, when I came across a dark brown wooden jewelry box with the *Irish Blessing* inscribed on the lid. As I opened it, I spotted a small claddagh ring tucked away inside. After confirming that my sisters didn't want it, I took it for myself and lovingly wear it to this day. The claddagh ring, a crowned heart offered by two hands, is full of symbolism. The heart stands for love, the crown for loyalty, and the hands for friendship. The design is named for the town where it originated, Claddagh, County Galway, in the province of Connacht. This popular Irish ring can indicate your marital or dating status by the way it is worn on your hand. Worn on your left hand with the heart pointing inward signals you're married; but if the heart points outward, you are engaged. Alternatively, wearing it on your right hand with the heart pointing outward means you are "available," and pointing inward warns you're in a relationship or "taken."

As I study the claddagh ring on my hand, I don't look at it as hardware signifying my status in a romantic relationship. It reminds me of my family, my mom and my dad, and the many generations before them, especially since my DNA map lights up like a Christmas tree over the northwestern corner of Connacht. I particularly see the oversized hands of my father offering me his big heart, not as a sweetheart but as a loving father, as my loyal friend and companion. I also feel his hands tugging at my own heart. His irresistible charm and smiling Irish eyes really could "steal your heart away." Without hesitation, I offered my steadfast daughterly love in return. This mutual self-donation sustained us as we journeyed through the last days of Frank's life in love, loyalty, and friendship.

When Irish Eyes are Smiling

There's a tear in your eye and I'm wondering why,
For it never should be there at all;
With such pow'r in your smile,
sure a stone you'd beguile,
So there's never a tear-drop should fall;
When your sweet lilting laughter's like some fairy song,
And your eyes twinkle bright as can be;
You should laugh all the while and all other times, smile,
And now smile a smile for me.

When Irish eyes are smiling,
Sure it's like a morn in Spring,
In the lilt of Irish laughter
You can hear the angels sing.
When Irish hearts are happy,
All the world seems bright and gay,
And when Irish eyes are smiling,
Sure, they steal your heart away.

Chauncey Olcott and George Graff, Jr.

Chapter 29

Anam Cara

The Irish use the term "Anam Cara" to describe a deep spiritual bond between two souls. Though the English translation would be "soul friend" or "soul mate," it doesn't refer to a married couple who have found their one true love, but names the connection between two people, at times on a subconscious level, that unleashes your true self. Some Irish consider an Anam Cara to be a spiritual midwife who accompanies a person passing from this life to the next.

Frank and I were blessed to share an Anam Cara relationship. Some of my fondest memories are our "walks around the lake" at the University of Notre Dame. During the last years Frank lived in Pennsylvania, I was working on a master's degree in liturgy from Notre Dame. For six summers I traveled to South Bend for a three-week semester, savoring the opportunity to study theology. I was what St. Anselm described as "faith, seeking understanding." In other words, I was seeking a deeper understanding for the God with whom I had fallen in love. Yet, I was so humbled to discover that God loves us first. "Before I formed you in the womb I knew you" (Jer 1:5). I had to let it settle into my bones that it wasn't I who was pursing God; it is God who is pursuing each and every one of us. "It was not you who chose me, but I who chose you" (Jn 15:16). We are just responding to God's call.

I devoured the reading assignments into the wee hours, and when the sun rose, I looked forward to attending daily Mass, followed by classes in the beautiful campus setting. There is something very special at Notre Dame; many claim that Notre Dame is the source and summit of what it means to be Irish Catholic in America. But for me the particularly special moments came in the late afternoon when I would take a break from my studies, leave my dorm room in Pasquerilla East Hall, and meander west across campus. Passing the "Stonehenge" fountain, I welcomed the damp breeze wafting from its rushing water then strolled by the statue of the Sacred Heart of Jesus, his arms outstretched toward the statue of his Blessed Mother, reigning over the entire campus from atop the Golden Dome. As if beckoned, I would continue into the beautiful Basilica of the Sacred Heart. The soothing cool air welcomed me in from the hot Indiana summer day; I felt drawn toward the warm swirling water in the baptismal font. Immersing my hands up to my wrist was so comforting I wanted to go deeper. Had it been a full immersion font, I might have been tempted to dive right in. Fortunately, it wasn't. Soaking in the font might have been grounds for expulsion from the university. As baptism leads to the Eucharist, I would process slowly down the center aisle towards the altar. Glimpses of the golden tabernacle tower brought again to mind that in this sublime space we take part in the "already not yet," where we celebrate the foretaste of the heavenly liturgy.[25] I would circle around the sanctuary to the back door and down the steps to the grotto, the heart of the university. Hewn into the hillside is a model of the miracle at Lourdes, with a statue of Bernadette kneeling beneath our Blessed Mother, the Immaculate Conception. In this ethereal space, permeated by the soothing scent of melting wax and flickering candlelight, I sensed that heaven and earth had touched.

I added one more lighted candle to the hundreds already burning there, each one representing a fervent prayer. Reverently I got down on my knees and prayed a rosary, as so many have done before. I prayed for my family, for all those in need, and that through the intercession of our Blessed Mother I might surrender my will for the will of God to let the incarnation continue in and through me, in the example of Mary's *fiat*.

As I rose from the kneeler and headed toward St. Mary's Lake, I would call Frank on my cell phone. Slowly circling the lake, I chatted with him, catching up on the blessings and burdens of the day.

First and foremost, I wanted a health update. "Dad, how are you feeling today?"

Never complaining, he inevitably answered, "Pretty good."

Predictably, he changed the subject. "How are your studies going? Did you finish reading chapters five through eight like you wanted to?"

I answered with painful honesty, "Ugh, how about chapters five through seven?

Frank cheered me on, "Well, keep at it, Riley!"

"Dad, did you know that Meister Eckhart said that 'God is nearer to me than I am to myself?' Does that make sense to you?"

"Oh, absolutely."

It was odd thinking how close I felt to Frank although he was physically fifteen hundred miles away. Why should I be so surprised? Saint Paul taught us that, "we, though many, are one body in Christ and individually parts of one another" (Rom 12:5). Jesus said, "Amen, I say to you, whatever you did for one of these least brothers of mine, you did for me" (Mt 25:40). We are the Church, members of the mystical Body of Christ, intimately connected to Christ, the head, *and* to our brothers and sisters in Christ.

Then I asked, "Did you study theology at King's College?"

"I did. I was a business major, but honestly, the theology classes were my favorite!"

"Hmm. I didn't know that."

At the end of a semester, I would continue on from Notre Dame to Mountain Top, since I was already halfway there. During my last summer at Notre Dame, and Frank's last summer in Mountain Top, with the grace of God, I passed my comprehensive exams. I graduated! According to the Notre Dame ritual all new theology graduates were treated to a celebratory dinner on the second floor of South Dining Hall. The traditional dessert, a large sheet cake with a giant green shamrock emblazoned right in the center, was a beacon for my weary eyes. After everyone had a slice, I noticed that the green shamrock was still there. I sidled up to the cake, looking longingly at it when an observant server asked me if I wanted a piece "to go." I'm embarrassed to admit how excited I was to bring that shamrock cake back to Mountain Top for Frank. I felt he had earned it too. Knowing the many things it symbolized, he relished every bite.

ST. BRIGID

Along with St. Patrick and St. Brendan, St. Brigid (421-525 AD) is a beloved patron saint of Ireland. One legend surrounding her life concerns St. Brigid's cross. The story goes that Brigid was called to the deathbed of a pagan chieftain who many claim was her own father. When he asked her about her Christian faith, she took rushes from the floor beside his bed and wove a cross to explain the

Paschal Mystery of Christ. Her evangelization so moved him that the chieftain agreed to convert to Christianity and before he died was baptized. St. Brigid's cross reminds us of the power of ministering at a deathbed. God never relents in seeking our salvation even up to our last breath. Perhaps St. Brigid, also the patron saint of midwives, was her father's Anam Cara. She had a deep appreciation for spiritual relationships and is quoted as having said "A person without an Anam Cara is like a body without a head." That is, one is never fully whole without an Anam Cara.

Not only can a caregiver spiritually support and evangelize the sick, but it is important to recognize the tremendous opportunity for dying Christians to witness their deep faith to caregivers, family, and friends. The witness of my father's desire for the sacraments and his continued prayer life in his last months testified to his faith and love of God, to his belief that there were higher things than his suffering here on earth. He was an inspiration to everyone around him, for in a powerful way he was a living witness that the sick can offer their suffering in union with Christ's for the salvation of the world.

JESUS AS OUR ANAM CARA

Though we may have the good fortune to connect in this life with another human being as our Anam Cara, Jesus is our true spiritual companion, our mystagogue, closer to us than we are to ourselves, walking with us through all our blessings and struggles. The scriptures reveal Jesus' accompaniment in good times and bad. Jesus joined with family and friends in a wedding celebration and came to their assistance when they faced the embarrassment of running out of wine (Jn 2:1-12). He enjoyed dining with his friends Mary and Martha (Lk 10:38-42) and grieved with them when their brother Lazarus died (Jn 11:1-44).

Pope Francis describes how Jesus accompanies missionaries—and indeed all Christians are missionaries— for through our baptism we are sent to bring Christ to others. "A true missionary, who never ceases to be a disciple, knows that Jesus walks with him, speaks to him, breathes with him, works with him. He senses Jesus alive with him in the midst of the missionary enterprise."[26]

Today Jesus accompanies us through the reception of the sacraments as Pope Leo the Great explained: "What was visible in our Savior has passed over into his mysteries."[27] Through the sacrament of the Anointing of the Sick, Jesus stands at our sick bed, just as he visited St. Peter's mother-in-law (Lk 4:38-39). Through the reception of the Eucharist as viaticum, the last sacrament of Christian life,[28] Jesus holds our hand at our death bed, just as he took Jairus' daughter by the hand (Mk 5:21-43).

Our relationship with Jesus far surpasses that of any human Anam Cara, for not only does he accompany us as we pass from this life to the next, but in laying down his life for us he promised that "Whoever eats my flesh and drinks my blood has eternal life, and I will raise him on the last day" (Jn 6:54). Those who accompany the dying, then, must point to our true Anam Cara, Jesus, just as St. Brigid did.

"Anam Cara" written in the ogham alphabet of Primitive Irish.

Prayer to St. Brigid of Ireland

Brigid,
You were a woman of peace.
You brought harmony where there was conflict.
You brought light to the darkness.
You brought hope to the downcast.

May the mantle of your peace cover
those who are troubled and anxious,
and may peace be firmly rooted
in our hearts and in our world.
Inspire us to act justly
and to reverence all God has made.

Brigid you were a voice for the wounded and the weary.
Strengthen what is weak within us.
Calm us into a quietness that heals and listens.
May we grow each day into greater wholeness
in mind, body and spirit.

Amen.

Chapter 30

The Turkey Meatloaf

Growing up in Mountain Top, we had few rules, no curfew, and cell phone tracking hadn't been invented. We had free reign to do whatever we wanted except for one nonnegotiable rule: mealtimes included anyone and everyone who was in our Mountain Top home. Whether you just stopped by for a visit, or to clean the toilet, a place was set for you at the table. It wasn't just a meal—it was an event, complete with placemats, cloth napkins, and homemade iced tea. At the kitchen table you were just as likely to sit next to your sister as you were to Mrs. Eroh, who cleaned; Chris, who cut grass; or Rob, who painted. We were equal. No one was better than anyone else.

So of course, when Frank's staff filled our house in San Diego, there was a place for everyone at the table. All were simultaneously equal and valued; everyone had an integral part in caring for Frank. Without everyone pitching in, Frank couldn't be here in our home.

Cooking wasn't a problem; I have always liked to cook, and I rallied to the cause. Admittedly, my standards were a bit low: no one goes hungry, and no one gets sick. But as the days turned into weeks, and weeks turned into months my enthusiasm waned a bit trying to balance meals, work, the household, and keeping the mini hospital running. Since Frank had diabetes, timing of the meals was a priority.

But then – the big idea arrived – the Holy Spirit helped me through yet again! Early one morning, I got out the crock-pot and filled it with enough turkey meatloaf to feed the entire clan and set off for work. I had to admit, I was really proud of myself. I stopped acknowledging the Holy Spirit and took all the credit. I had it all organized, I was doing it all! I had that balancing act down to a fine art.

Then at 10:00 a.m. I noticed a text from Brian, Frank's CNA. My heart skipped a beat. Something was up with Frank. But then I realized it wasn't about Frank, it was the meatloaf.

"I see you left food in a crock-pot; did you want it turned on?"

"Oh, yeah, thanks Brian, go ahead and turn it on."

A bit red-faced, I winced and said to myself, it's OK Noreen, don't worry, it's just a little glitch. You got this.

After work, I arrived home just in time to get the dinner on the table. Turkey meatloaf, check! Salad, check! Sweet! Then the trouble started.

Frank asked, "So, Noreen, what is this?"

"Dad, it's turkey meatloaf."

"Hmmm. . . . This isn't one of your better meals, you know."

"Oh. OK."

"I don't think we should keep this in the rotation."

Oh dear. That was definitely a thumbs down.

I looked at all the faces around the table and I could see that they were all in agreement. And then it happened. Peter spoke up. "Frank, I would be happy to cook for you. What would you like?"

The bells rang, the angels sang, and the gates of heaven opened. Frank's eyes widened, his dimples deepened and the love triangle between the father, the son-in-law, and the barbecue was set into motion. The crock-pot was quickly upgraded to a Big Green Egg and the turkey meatloaf gave way to large slabs of beef, pork, and lamb. We turned into a slaughterhouse/smokehouse. The coyotes howled louder with each passing night, and Frank needed to go up a size in all his clothes. It got to the point where the doctor started giving the lecture.

"Fist size portions of protein!"

My fist or Frank's fist? Frank's fist is probably worth two pounds of meat.

"Frank should be losing weight, not gaining it."

But how do you do that? Do you do that? Eating was one of the remaining activities that gave Frank joy. How do you take someone off eating food that he loves? The doctor explained the situation to Frank. We could have enforced the doctor's will. Since he was bedridden there would be no midnight refrigerator raids. Instead, out of respect for Frank, we let him make the decision. It validated that he had dignity and deserved to be treated as such. And so, the food orgy continued.

The turkey meatloaf was a big turning point in our household. Peter enjoyed the meal ministry to Frank. Frank enjoyed collaborating with Peter on the menus. I was able to take something BIG off my plate, literally. It was an answer to my prayers. But looking back, I think there was only one problem with it. I wish I had made that turkey meatloaf sooner!

Ask and You Shall Receive

"Ask and it will be given to you;
seek and you will find;
knock and the door will be opened to you.
For everyone who asks, receives;
and the one who seeks, finds;
and to the one who knocks, the door will be opened.
Which one of you would hand his son a stone
when he asks for a loaf of bread,
or a snake when he asks for a fish?
If you then, who are wicked,
know how to give good gifts to your children,
how much more will your heavenly Father
give good things to those who ask him."

(Mt 7:7-11)

Chapter 31

The Cousins Come to Visit

Ever since we moved to California thirty years ago, I had dreamed of Aunt Nancy and Uncle Johnny coming for a visit. Aunt Nancy was my mother's only sibling and best friend, and Uncle Johnny was Frank's best friend and the brother he never had. As high school sweethearts, Aunt Nancy and Uncle Johnny double dated with mom and dad and the foursome remained close all their lives. Aunt Nancy and Uncle Johnny were the parents of my treasured cousins, Lyn and Sue, identical twins, and their three younger brothers, Pat, Greg, and Dave. Every Thanksgiving, we would pile into the Chrysler on Wednesday night, with mom and dad up front and my two sisters, me, and Nana praying the rosary squeezed into the back. We drove down to South Jersey to spend the holiday. Every Easter they made the reverse journey, to be with us in Mountain Top. Cousins filled the beds with some even strewn about the floor. You had to tip-toe over curly heads on pillows and little bodies tucked under blankets. Holiday meals promised the Thanksgiving turkey or the Easter ham, Mrs. Suttman's potatoes (the family favorite cheesy potato casserole she left as her legacy), Jell-o molds, and pâté on Triscuits. We never missed a Thanksgiving parade that brought Santa to town, and we found every Easter basket in record time.

After the two couples bought a cottage together on the Jersey shore, we enjoyed summer vacations with our cousins. We treasure fond memories of catching fish on Uncle Johnny's boat, *The Sea Wall*, and chasing crabs down the dock. As the years passed by and we were blessed with our own children, we made sure they vacationed at the cottage too. We wanted the next generation to experience the love and close bond that we had always enjoyed. Those days were filled with good memories: early morning fishing trips, walks along the bay hunting horseshoe crabs, ice-cold gin and tonics on a hot summer evening, and late-night chats on the back porch.

I wanted to return my aunt and uncle's warm hospitality and spoil them with a stiff happy hour cocktail followed by a sumptuous dinner just as they had lavished upon me for so many years. But their visit did not turn out as I had hoped or imagined. Lyn and Sue, along with Lyn's teenage son, Kevin, brought Aunt Nancy and Uncle Johnny to California to say good-bye to Frank. They needed closure. They had left mom's funeral not knowing that Frank would move to California, and they wanted to be with him one last time. Lyn and Sue operated as one person; when one started a sentence, the other finished it and would end with the same giggle. Kevin was there for moral and physical support. His big strong arms could lift anything, and his winning smile could calm anyone down. It took the three of them, Lyn, Sue, and Kevin to manage Aunt Nancy and Uncle Johnny as they flew from New Jersey to California.

In the early stages of dementia, Aunt Nancy was getting more confused. We had hoped she would grasp the reality of this trip, but I lowered my expectations as she walked into my house and exclaimed, "Oh, I love what you've done with the lobby!" When I asked Aunt Nancy if I could get her a cup of coffee, she looked bewildered and asked, "Oh, do you work here?" My heart sank. It was difficult to see my fun-loving Aunt this way, but I was grateful that she was still alive. She reminded me so much of my mom, I just had to hold her close, accept her as she was, and love her.

Uncle Johnny always had a reputation for enjoying a drink now and then, but his recent bout of health issues worried the twins and they wanted him to curtail his intake of alcohol. This put me in the middle. In one ear Uncle Johnny would whisper, "Noreen, can you get me a drink? Just a short whiskey?" with the twins whispering in the other, "Noreen, please don't give dad a drink. He should not be drinking now; his health is not good."

What was I to do?

What did I do? I caved. I became the enabler. How do you say "no" to someone who has lost his sister-in-law, recognizes his best friend is dying, and worst of all, day by day is losing his wife to dementia? He may not admit it, but he knows. And yes, his health is failing too.

As Aunt Nancy, thinking she was in a hotel, guarded her purse and curiously moved things from the kitchen into her bedroom, Uncle Johnny pulled up a chair next to dad's hospital bed to reminisce. When Uncle Johnny went to lie down to rest, I sat with dad to see how he was handling this. Frank looked at me and, nodding in Uncle Johnny's direction, said, "That poor bugger is not good. I don't think he has long to live."

When Uncle Johnny got up from his nap, he pulled me aside and said, "Noreen, Frank's not good. You know he doesn't have long now."

The sadness surrounded us like a thick early morning fog.

When Greg brought Christina over to meet Aunt Nancy and Uncle Johnny it became another test of her patience with our family. Uncle Johnny loved to tell jokes and always took advantage of a new face to retell some of his old favorites. He was in rare form and launched right into the one about Pat and Peg.

Peg walks into the front room where Pat is sitting watching television.

"Pat, I'm going down to the doctor's now for my sixty-year-old checkup."

Pat replies, "OK, Peg I'll see ya after."

After a couple of hours, Peg returns to find Pat still sitting in front of the television and says, "Pat, I'm back now."

Pat replies, not taking his eyes off the television, "Well, what did the doctor have to say, there Peg?"

"It's good news, Pat. He said I have the legs of a thirty-year-old."

"Did he now? Harrumph."

"Yes, and he said that I have the flat firm abdomen of a forty-year-old."

Pat, still looking at the TV, says, "Well, how about that now?"

Peg continues, "He said I have the sharp mind of a fifty-year-old."

Pat gives a frown and says, "Well, yeah, sure Peg. But what did he say about your sixty-year-old arse?"

Peg replies, "Well, nothing, Pat, your name never came up at all."

Christina smiled politely, while I prayed that she would think kindly of us all.

Peter and I thought the best way to celebrate—no, to redeem—this visit was to take everyone out to lunch in La Jolla, at a fancy restaurant that has an upper deck with a breathtaking view of the Pacific Ocean. The hostess assured me that the restaurant was accessible because they had an elevator. I confidently hired a wheelchair van to drive Frank and me to the restaurant while Peter drove the rest of the family to meet us there. When we arrived, the driver extended the lift from the back of the van so it cantilevered three feet over Prospect Street. He cautiously wheeled Frank onto the lift and pushed the button to make it descend. When the lift didn't move, he grimaced and said, "The switch isn't working to lower the lift down to the street level. I'll have to call the home office."

I calmly responded, "OK, but can you move my dad back into the van, so he isn't suspended indefinitely over the street?"

"Oh, Oh, yeah. I can do that."

It took a good ten minutes for the driver to get the switch to operate. He tried to hide the fact that the switch was unplugged. Isn't that always the first thing you check when something doesn't work? Anyway, now that Frank was on the street level, all that remained was taking the elevator up to join the family on the top level of the restaurant. I scanned the sidewalk to find the elevator, but only saw a very small chair lift. I asked the parking attendants where the elevator was, and they pointed to the lift. Great. It was like a small, motorized box that went up one level. I tried to squeeze the wheelchair in, but it was too wide. I studied Frank's chair and realized that it had rims screwed onto the wheels to move yourself manually. I thought, if I could just unscrew one of the rims, the chair would just fit into the lift. But where would I get a Phillips head screwdriver in the middle of swanky La Jolla? I spotted a delivery truck down the block and ran to ask the driver if he had a screwdriver I could borrow. Now, it's not every day that you would get stopped on the street in La Jolla for a screwdriver, but somehow I looked legitimate and not like I was pulling some prank. Sweating bullets, I unscrewed the rim, returned the screwdriver, and was ready to launch Frank in the lift. But, oh, my Lord, he still didn't fit. OK. OK. Just see if you can borrow the screwdriver again. The delivery truck driver at this point didn't need to assess whether I was crazy or not. That had already been established, but I also proved that I would reliably return the screwdriver. One more try. Frank just sat there patiently and silently as I took off the other rim, returned the screwdriver, and then SUCCESS! Frank fit into the lift.

But now I needed to make a leap of faith. Fortunately, by now I had become well practiced at that. Since I couldn't fit into the lift with Frank, I had to send him up without me and pray to God he would arrive, not get stuck between floors, like on the wheelchair van. So, I closed the lift door, said a prayer, pushed the button, ran up the flight of steps, and met the lift on the next floor. And there, with a smile on his face, was Frank! Do I laugh or do I cry?

As I pushed him into the restaurant to meet the rest of the family, everyone stood up and cheered Frank's arrival! I think I was numb. I couldn't believe we had just made it through all that. The lunch was lovely, and the ride back home was uneventful. Thanks be to God.

The next day, I finally had the courage to bring up the fiasco with Frank. I said, "Dad, I am so sorry about the whole mess at the restaurant with the lift on the van getting stuck and having to take the rims off the wheelchair one by one to squeeze you into that tiny elevator."

With a puzzled look on his face he asked, "What are you talking about?" He shook his head and said, "I don't know what you mean. That was the best part of the whole lunch."

Seeing the world through Frank's eyes was truly illuminating. Keep at it, Riley!

Aunt Nancy and I always loved to sing the old Irish songs together. So, when I got out my guitar so we could sing a few of the tunes for old times' sake, the most amazing thing happened. I only needed to start the song out and she could sing every word! She remembered the lyrics even better than I did. We sang "Danny Boy" and "Granny's Old Armchair," songs that she taught me when I was a little girl. The same songs that Mom Conway taught her when she was little. Obviously, it was time for me to pass them down as well.

The time together with my cousins was bittersweet. We were glad that we could support each other to share a few laughs, for certainly there were going to be some tough times ahead. It was painful to see Aunt Nancy, Uncle Johnny, and Frank together without mom. But the three of them were very strong. Their *faith* and *hope* in the Lord were very strong. They set a powerful example for all of us to follow.

Granny's Old Armchair

Oh my granny she, at the age of eighty-three,
One day in May was taken ill and died
And after she was dead, the will of course was read
By the lawyers as we all stood by his side.
To my sisters it was found she had left a hundred pounds
And the same unto my brother I declare.
But when it came to me, the lawyer said I see
Granny only left the old armchair.

How they tittered, how they chaffed
How my brothers and my sisters laughed
When they heard the lawyer declare
Granny only left to you the old armchair.

Well, one evening after tea,
She was seated on my knee and the seat it fell upon the floor.
And what to my surprise, I saw before my eyes,
Notes worth ten thousand pounds or more.
When my brother heard of this, the fellow I confess
Went nearly wild with rage and tore his hair!
I only laughed at him, and said, "unto you, Jim,
Don't you wish you had the old armchair?"

John Read

꧁

Chapter 32

The Anointing of the Sick

B orn in 1930, Frank—and those of his generation—
could be frightened if a priest came to their sick bed,
since his arrival signaled that you didn't have long to
live. Families waited to call the priest until their loved ones
were about to take their last breath, which unfortunately
always seemed to be in the middle of the night. The sacrament he administered had the ominous name "Extreme
Unction," which sounded like something that might kill you
even if your disease didn't. It was "extreme" in the sense
that it was received *in extremis,* or at the point of death
and "unction" referred to anointing with holy oils.

Today, however, the sacrament is known as the
Anointing of the Sick. The Second Vatican Council liturgical reforms gave the sacrament a more fitting name and
clarified that it should be celebrated not only at the point
of death but when a member of the faithful begins to be
in danger of death from sickness or old age.[29] A "person
may [also] be anointed before surgery whenever a serious
illness is the reason for the surgery. Elderly people may
be anointed if they have become notably weakened even
though no serious illness is present."[30] Death need not be
imminent, in fact, it is best to not wait too long since sacraments are celebrated only for the living, not for the dead.
If the priest arrives after a loved one has died, the family is

disappointed to learn that it is too late—he cannot anoint a deceased body. Instead, he would say the Prayers for the Dead that are included in the rites for PCS.[31]

Through the Anointing of the Sick "the Church supports the sick in their struggle against illness and continues Christ's messianic work of healing."[32] It is the Church's response to the command attested to by St. James:

> Is anyone among you sick? He should summon the presbyters of the church, and they should pray over him and anoint [him] with oil in the name of the Lord, and the prayer of faith will save the sick person, and the Lord will raise him up. If he has committed any sins, he will be forgiven.

> (Jas 5:14-15)

The grace of the sacrament of the Anointing of the Sick can have manifold effects for our loved ones when administered at the time of a life-threatening illness or old age. The sacrament unites the sick to the passion of Christ not only for their own benefit but for the whole Church. They also receive peace and courage to endure their suffering, forgiveness of sin, restoration of health if it is conducive for their salvation, and preparation for passing over to eternal life.[33] Looking back on a Thanksgiving weekend, about fifteen years before Frank came to live with us, it was clear that he needed the grace of the sacrament at that moment.

My parents and my sisters with their families had traveled to San Diego to spend the holiday with my family. Frank suddenly fell quite ill and ended up in the hospital, where each day his symptoms worsened. The doctors were baffled, unable to diagnose or treat his illness. Concerned about his rapidly deteriorating condition, I wanted Frank to receive the Anointing of the Sick. Trying not to alarm him, I softly whispered, "Hey Dad, what do you think about a priest coming by to give you an anointing? It's not called Extreme Unction anymore; it's now understood to be a sacrament of the sick."

He seemed agreeable and even perked up a bit, "OK, that sounds good."

I was so relieved that he didn't ask "How long do I have?" or "Do you think I'm going to make it?"

I calmly replied, "All right, I'll see if I can make that happen."

I reached out to our pastor, Msgr. Harnett. "Monsignor, would you be able to come to the hospital to anoint my dad? He is here visiting from Pennsylvania and took ill. The doctors don't know what is wrong and he keeps getting worse every day."

The monsignor, from County Kerry, answered in his thick brogue, "All right, Noreen, I can be there in an hour."

I relayed the good news to Frank. "Dad, do you remember Msgr. Harnett, our pastor? He will be here in an hour."

Frank raised his eyebrows, nodded his head, and said, "Oh, good."

He looked around the room and asked, "Does anyone have a comb?" We were all shocked.

What? Suddenly, he's worried about how he looks? From that moment on, Frank started to recover. It was as if Msgr. Harnett was already praying for Frank as he made his way to the hospital.

As promised, our pastor arrived and invited all the family present, my mother, my sisters, and me to gather around close by Frank's bedside to make our prayer of faith, in a spirit of trust, that the Lord will raise Frank up and save him (Jas 5:15).

In silence, Msgr. Harnett gently laid his hands upon Frank's head, praying for the Holy Spirit to come upon him. Jesus had laid his hands upon the sick (Lk 4:40) and directed the apostles to go into the world to do the same (Mk 16:18). Through his ordination to the priesthood, Msgr. Harnett is likewise commissioned to minister to Frank. He is anointing in the name of Christ and with the power of Christ that Frank will be strengthened to fight against the physical and spiritual effects of the illness.

Monsignor anointed Frank with *Oleum Infirmorum*, the Oil of the Infirm that the bishop blessed at the diocesan Chrism Mass. First, he anointed his forehead, saying:

> "Through this holy anointing
> may the Lord in his love and mercy help you
> with the grace of the Holy Spirit.
> Amen."

Then he anointed Frank's hands, saying:

> "May the Lord who frees you from sin save you and raise you up. Amen."[34]

After reciting the Lord's Prayer, we were all invited to receive the Body of Christ. In this compelling moment, our faith that the Eucharist will bring us to everlasting life provided great comfort and reminded us that one day we will be together again. "Whoever eats my flesh and drinks my blood has eternal life, and I will raise him on the last day" (Jn 6:54).

Thankfully, Frank rebounded from his illness quickly and a few days later was discharged from the hospital. In addition to Frank's recovery, my sisters, my mother, and I seemed to have received graces as well. The sacrament comforts those who are close to the sick with the message of hope, and as a result we had a greater sense of peace and harmony in dealing with Frank's illness and all its related issues. We were a living example of St. Paul's observation that, if one part of the Body of Christ suffers, all parts suffer with it; if one part is honored, all the parts share its joy (1 Cor. 12:26).

Fortunately, the Anointing of the Sick may be repeated: ". . . when the sick person recovers after being anointed and, at a later time becomes sick again; [or] when during the same illness the condition of the sick person becomes more serious. In the case of a person who is chronically ill, or elderly and in a weakened condition, the sacrament of anointing may be repeated when in the pastoral judgment of the priest the condition of the sick person warrants the repetition of the sacrament."[35] And so, back in Mountain Top when Frank's health deteriorated again, mom was able to call for the priest to administer the sacrament. Then, after Frank moved to San Diego, I could call Msgr. Harnett to anoint Frank again. Frank received the sacrament with gratitude and peace, and my family was blessed with grace to sustain us as we cared for Frank.

Blessing of the Oil of the Sick

O God, Father of all consolation,
who willed to heal the infirmities of the weak
through your Son,
listen favorably to the prayer of faith:
send forth from the heavens, we pray,
your Holy Spirit, the Paraclete,
upon this oil in all its richness,
which you have graciously brough forth
from the verdant tree to restore the body,
so that by your holy blessing +
everyone anointed with this oil,
as a safeguard for body, soul, and spirit
may be freed from all pain,
all infirmity,
and all sickness.
May your holy oil, O Lord,
be blessed by you for our sake
in the name of Jesus Christ our Lord.
Who lives and reigns with you for ever and ever.
Amen[36]

Chapter 33

I Want to Go Home

Carrickfergus

I wish I was in Carrickfergus
only for nights in Ballygran
I would swim over the deepest ocean
the deepest ocean
for my love to find
but the sea is wide and I cannot cross over
nor do I have any wings to fly
if I could find me a handsome boatman
to ferry me over to my love and die

F rank, the fighting Irishman, didn't know how to let up. He was the "Keep at it, Riley!" full-code, no DNR warrior that would defy all odds! I continued to be his advocate and ensured that "giving him a chance" included offering all life-extending options. Frank had the uncanny ability to remain optimistic. It wasn't my place to question, only to support. I knew I just needed to meet him where he was at.

Sergio scheduled trips to the cardiologist and the pulmonologist to keep an eye on Frank's heart and lungs. During one visit to the pulmonologist Frank asked the doctor, "Considering the current state of my lungs, would I be able to fly? I need to go back to Pennsylvania to clean out my house and sell it." I was shocked. I thought I might need CPR. I was impressed that he wanted to do it, and so happy that he felt well enough even to consider it, yet I was baffled that he didn't comprehend the seriousness of his illness. The doctor, carefully weighing his words, cautiously replied, "I don't see how flying would be a problem for your lungs."

Frank seemed relieved, and I could almost hear the wheels turning in his head as he calculated how he was going to pull it off.

Later that day, during our nightly prayer time, I casually said, "Don't worry about your house, Dad. We don't have to deal with that right now." We both knew he was good at reading between the lines. It was my way of telling him, without saying it out loud, that I would take care of it after he died. It was better to leave it like that. I wanted to take away all the anxiety that I possibly could.

We were able to manage Frank's care with only a few bumps in the road, like the night I woke up with a start, sensing that something was wrong. I went down to Frank's room to find blood running out of his catheter line instead of urine. On Dr. N.'s advice we went took an ambulance to the hospital. It got sorted out in a few days' time and Frank was sent home with a peripherally inserted central catheter (PICC line). The PICC line delivered drugs through a flexible tube extending from a port in the arm to the heart. Here was the catch: the drugs had to be administered through the port either by a family member or a registered nurse. That meant me! I had to do it. Though I had risen above my aversion to nursing, I had not tackled my anxiety about doing something that could harm Frank. Don't you think making a mistake inserting drugs into a line that goes directly to his heart could be one of those things? But it needed to be done and we didn't have a registered nurse, so I learned how to do it and prayed even more. I was very methodical about the procedure, and it all went fine. Thanks be to God!

One afternoon, Frank started struggling to breathe, so I administered a nebulizer treatment, but it didn't improve anything. I turned up the mix of O_2 in his oxygenator and gave him some lorazepam to calm his anxiety, but that didn't help either. I tried another nebulizer treatment, to no avail. I had to call 911. The ambulance arrived in record time. They put Frank on portable oxygen, gave him a shot of epinephrine and whisked him to the hospital, I followed in my car, praying and calling my sisters to let them know what was going on. Upon arrival, Frank's vital signs were not good, and he was admitted into the intensive care unit (ICU). Fortunately, Ellyn was able to get down to San Diego quickly to be with Frank. Once again, we called for a priest. Our associate pastor arrived and to prevent the spread of infection suited up in bright yellow personal protective equipment, PPE. Despite the gown and mask, he soldiered on to administer the sacrament.

Our family surrounded the hospital bed and as Father asked everyone to place their hands on Frank he suddenly noticed, "Oh, you already have your hands on him." Though Frank had been anointed before, sensing his sharp decline, we welcomed the deeply prayerful and comforting ritual for him and for us once more.

As Father was leaving, Ellyn, the nurse, reminded him, "Don't forget to take everything off before you leave."

Father turned with a start. . .

Ellyn giggled, "Oh—sorry! I mean the yellow protective garb—everything that's not black."

The team of doctors at the ICU met with Ellyn and me as they made their early morning rounds. The news was not good. They reported that his heart and lungs were unstable and not responding to any treatment.

I asked, "Can you discharge him so we can just take care of him at home?"

The lead ICU doctor replied, "Unfortunately, he is too unstable. He might not make it home, and since he is full code, even if he made it home, he would end up right back here. Have you thought of hospice?"

"No. Frank doesn't want hospice."

"What about palliative care?"

"I'm not sure what that means. Is that an option?"

I was grateful that the hospital staff took the time to explain the difference between palliative care and hospice care. Anyone at any age with a serious illness can receive palliative care. It focuses on symptom management and quality of life and can include life-extending treatment such as chemotherapy or radiation. Hospice care, however, is for patients that are expected to live six months or less and prefer to forgo life extending treatments. Because curative measures could be painful and futile, the illness is allowed to run its natural course. Hospice care includes twenty-four-hour physician coverage, a once-a-week nurse visit, and all medical equipment necessary for comfort and to ease the pain. If Frank wanted to go home, he would have to be under hospice care.

Even though Frank was very groggy, he opened his eyes and asked me when he could go home. This was a difficult message to relay, but I could only tell the truth.

"Well, Dad, the doctors say that if they release you, you'll be right back here. Your heart and lungs are unstable." He nodded off to sleep again, but I could tell that he understood.

I left his room for a quick bite to eat. Upon my return, Frank looked at me in a way he had never done before, and said very clearly and directly,

"I want to go home. Take me home."

"OK, Dad, I'm here to do whatever you want me to do. I'll go get a nurse to make the arrangements."

This was a pivotal moment for all of us. My father was ready to let go, let God. He was still so strong, yet I had to be stronger. I had to let go, let God too.

The hospice nurse came in to speak with Frank.

"Frank, I understand that you want to go home now."

In a loud strong voice, Frank said, "YES, I DO!"

"Do you understand that we will just be keeping you comfortable at home?"

"YES, I DO!"

The nurse nodded her head and left to make the arrangements for hospice care.

The man that had "kept at it, Riley," the man that had done everything his way, was now planning his trip home. It was a sign, not of weakness, but of strength. He was ready to go home. Frank spoke loudly, clearly, and emphatically as if he wanted to be sure I would remember that he was the one that had said it. This was his decision. There was to be no burden on me or my sisters. It was clear that he wanted to go home! My big, strong, fighting Irish daddy was ready to go home to God. Again, we were meeting him where he was at.

The nurse came back to let us know that the doctors didn't think he would make it home in an ambulance without oxygen. Unfortunately, an ambulance with oxygen wouldn't be available until the next day. Agreeing to wait,

Ellyn and I spent the night sharing a fold-out chair in Frank's room just to be near him.

Early the next morning, Chris came to the hospital and asked if we wanted a priest. Of course, we said yes, so Chris arranged for Fr. C. to come. I will be forever grateful for Father leading us in the Commendation of the Dying, a prayer that was as much for us as it was for Frank.

> Holy Mary, Mother of God, pray for him
> Holy angels of God, pray for him
> St. John the Baptist, pray for him
> St. Joseph, pray for him
> St. Peter and St. Paul, pray for him
> St. Patrick, pray for him
> St. Brendan, pray for him
> St. Brigid, pray for him
>
> I commend you, my dear brother, Frank, to almighty God,
> and entrust you to your Creator.
> May you return to him who formed you from the dust of the earth.
> May holy Mary, the angels, and all the saints
> come to meet you as you go forth from this life.
> May Christ who was crucified for you bring you freedom and peace.
> May Christ who died for you,
> admit you into his garden of paradise.
> May Christ, the true Shepherd,
> acknowledge you as one of his flock.
> May he forgive all your sins,
> and set you among those he has chosen.
> May you see your Redeemer face to face,
> and enjoy the vision of God for ever. Amen.[37]

As the orderlies started to roll Frank's gurney out to the medical transport to go home, he briefly opened his eyes and I quickly said, "I love you, Dad."

With his eyes closed, he mouthed back to me his last words, "I love you, too."

Ellyn and I traveled nervously with Frank in the transport when, halfway home, Ellyn noticed that Frank seemed to be under duress. She asked the respiratory therapist to turn up his oxygen, when she remarked, "Oh, the respirator isn't plugged in."

REALLY?

I felt a huge sense of relief as we brought Frank over the threshold; we made it!! He was home, yet on his way to be home with God and his wife Joan. All this while I had been bottling my emotions to stay strong for Frank, but I felt myself starting to buckle until I laid eyes upon my two dear friends, Joan and Denise, waiting with open arms and hearts. They had brought love, prayers, and food, that gave us renewed strength to carry us through the home stretch.

We had such mixed feelings. We were sad that Frank's time on earth was coming to a close, yet we felt a sense of comfort knowing that he was journeying home to God to rest in peace, that his struggle with illness would soon come to an end. We got out the hymnals and sang every comforting song we knew as Frank's granddaughters gathered around to comfort him with soothing caresses and assure him that he wasn't alone.

When a homebound minister arrived with the Blessed Sacrament in a pyx my heart lightened. I would now be able to celebrate the Rite of Viaticum. The celebration of the eucharist as viaticum, food for the passage through death to eternal life, is the sacrament proper to the dying Christian. It is the completion and crown of the Christian life on this earth, signifying that the Christian follows the Lord to eternal glory and the banquet of the heavenly kingdom. "The sacrament of the anointing of the sick should be celebrated at the beginning of a serious illness. Viaticum, celebrated when death is close, will then be better understood as the last sacrament of Christian life."[38]

Since a priest or deacon wasn't available, as a lay minister, I was able to lead the celebration of the rite. It was my honor and privilege as Frank's human *Anam Cara* through these last years, to be the one to give him the Eucharist as Viaticum, the food for the journey, which is Jesus, his true *Anam Cara.*

As Frank received Holy Communion for the last time, I felt that we had done our job. We had sent him on his way home, to the threshold of heaven, as he had asked. Just before midnight we stood close by, praying the rosary, as he drew his last breath. The angels came to take him home.

I gently tucked Frank in a blanket that boldly displayed the Fighting Irish Leprechaun, the symbol he loved so much. I placed a lit candelabra at his head and at his feet and dimmed the overhead lights further. He had competed well; he had finished the race; he had kept the faith (2 Tm 4:7).

I poured a shot of Jameson for everyone—our family, and our caregivers. We raised our glasses to Frank and shared treasured Frank stories until the early morning hours. After everyone went to bed, I stayed *a-wake* by Frank's side, in prayer, all through the rest of the night. If anyone deserved an Irish wake, it was Frank.

I Am the Bread of Life

Amen, amen, I say to you,
whoever believes has eternal life.
I am the bread of life.
Your ancestors ate the manna in the desert,
but they died;
this is the bread that comes down from heaven
so that one may eat it and not die.
I am the living bread that came down from heaven;
whoever eats this bread will live forever;
and the bread that I will give is my flesh for the life of the world.

(Jn 6:47-51)

Chapter 34

The Second Wake

I made the arrangements to have Frank's body trans-
ported to Mountain Top so all our family and friends
back East could celebrate the Catholic Funeral Rites,
just as we had done for mom. The vigil would be at the
Mountain Top Funeral Home, the funeral Mass at St.
Jude's, and the Committal at St. Mary's Cemetery. But
wait, not so fast. . . What if we had an Irish wake in our
house in Mountain Top? Wouldn't that be perfect for
Frank? He hadn't been in his home since October, eight
months ago, and the last time was for his wife's funeral.
We would be able to gather with everyone in an informal
setting surrounded by our childhood memories. Since we
were going to sell the house right after the funeral, this
would be very special. Oh, and did I mention you could
have a cocktail right at the wake instead of out of the
trunk of a car in the parking lot?

While Mari and Ellyn and I were discussing the pros
and cons of the "house wake," it occurred to us that getting
the coffin into the house might be a challenge. So, I called
one of the local builders, a classmate of mine at St. Jude's
Elementary School.

"Joe. We want to have a wake for my dad in our house,
but I can't figure out how to get the coffin in. We have a
sliding door in the back but it's not wide enough."

"Noreen, that's not a problem, we can just pop off the sliding door and you'll get right in."

"That's terrific, would you be able to send us an invoice?"

"Oh, don't worry about that. We would just be happy to take care of it for you."

Did I really forget how nice Mountain Top people are?

But then another dilemma arose. A lawyer suggested that since our house wasn't accessible, people could hurt themselves getting in and might sue us. Wait a minute, aren't these the same nice Mountain Top people we were just talking about? Who would go after us in a personal injury lawsuit? The sure way to know would be to say an Irish Blessing: "May those who love us, love us; and those who don't love us, may God turn their hearts; and if He doesn't turn their hearts, may he turn their ankles, so we'll know them by their limping." It was decided that the prayer wasn't quite good enough, that we should have our guests sign waivers instead. Well, let's think about that.

Either way we still had to go to the Mountain Top Funeral Home to arrange for the coffin and the rest of the funeral plans. Mari and Ellyn and I were talking with George, the funeral director, when Mari brought up a serious question. "Do you remember how concerned dad always was about not looking like he was stuffed in a coffin?"

I shook my head no, but Ellyn replied, "Yeah, I do. He mentioned that at every wake. He would particularly point out the ones that were on the heavier side and say, 'Now, don't let me look like that! Look at their arms spilling out.'"

I tried not to visualize that and just asked what seemed to be a reasonable question: "Do you have any extra-large caskets?"

Everything in Frank's life was extra-large, why not his coffin?

George replied matter-of-factly, "That's not a problem. We can go ahead and order an extra-large coffin."

Changing the subject, I asked my sisters, "Have you thought about prayer cards for dad?"

Mari suggested, "What about the Prayer of St. Francis?" We all easily agreed to that. And then I asked, "Would you be OK with St. Patrick on the front?"

Nods all around. We had the prayer card done.

"I'll make a stop down at St. Mary's Cemetery to make sure we are all squared away there."

I stepped into the office at St. Mary's. "Hi, Charles. I'm Noreen McInnes. My mom was buried in the double-depth plot back in October. My dad recently passed away and we want to bury him above her."

Somehow this all seemed easier the second time around. I wouldn't have to go into all the double depth details this time. Or did I?

"Say, Charles. One more thing. It looks like my dad will need an extra-large coffin. Is that a problem?"

Wide-eyed, Charles gulped and said, "Oh that's definitely a problem. Only a regular-sized casket will fit in a double decker plot."

"OK. So, do I have this right? Its either a regular-sized casket or another plot, right?"

Charles nodded. "Right!"

"Hmm. All righty then. I'll have to get back with you."

Why is nothing easy? I asked Mari and Ellyn to meet me back at The Mountain Top Funeral Home to discuss this with George. "Keep at it, Riley!"

"George, in order to fit in his cemetery plot, we'll have to bury Frank in a regular-sized casket. But we need to honor Frank's wishes and not stuff him into a casket that's too small for him. What do you suggest?"

George pondered for a minute. "We could have the extra-large casket for the wake and then transfer him to the regular casket for the funeral Mass and burial. No one would know."

Thinking we may have found a plausible solution, I asked a follow-up question, "So could we just rent the extra-large casket if we don't need to use it after the wake?"

All his life Frank bought and sold cars just to satisfy his need to haggle. None of his offspring could resist a good haggling opportunity.

A bit shocked, George responded, "Unfortunately, Pennsylvania state laws prohibit renting caskets."

Well, that may be true, or it may not be true, but I wasn't giving up,

"Can you give us a better price if we are buying two caskets? I'm not suggesting a 'buy one get one' deal, but maybe you could do better than full price for both?"

Just then, a man in work clothes walked in and announced, "Can I get some help here?"

George, a bit ruffled by this interruption, replied, "How can I help you?"

"Well, I have this oversized casket on my truck that looks like it's for several people. I can't get that off by myself."

Mari, Ellyn, and I exchanged knowing glances. It looked like Frank's extra-large casket had arrived in short order!

George left to sort things out with the delivery, giving us a few minutes to talk things through.

I sighed, "I guess two caskets makes it a deal breaker to have the wake in the house. How would that work? Keep the spare casket in the kitchen or a bedroom? Talk about a conversation piece!"

Mari and Ellyn just rolled their eyes at me.

When George returned, he had a suggestion. "What if we put Frank in the smaller casket and then you can decide if it looks OK or not? The only catch is that we can't do that until late in the day tomorrow and that doesn't leave us much time to make the adjustments."

We agreed to that plan, which meant holding the wake at the funeral home, not at the house. I called St. Mary's Cemetery to let them know that Frank would be in a regular-sized casket and that we could go ahead and use the family plot.

Back at the house, we discussed the possibility of the extra-large casket for the wake and what that would look like. We were imagining the raised extra-wide lid looming large over dad. We decided that such a big blank backdrop would look very imposing. Haley, Ellyn's daughter, was a graphic designer. She suggested softening it up a bit by stringing carnations dyed in the colors of the Irish flag across the lid. Frank, of course, would be quite pleased with that. The five granddaughters quickly got to work on that project.

Mari, Ellyn, and I started to reminisce about dyed carnations. Every St. Patrick's Day, the greatest day of the year, Frank would buy his wife and each of his daughters a corsage of green carnations in honor of the patron saint of Ireland. It seemed logical that all the family should wear green carnations for the funeral Mass, corsages for the daughters and granddaughters and boutonnieres for the sons-in-law, grandson, and of course, Frank! But we couldn't stop there. We couldn't resist buying all the men kelly green ties to go with their boutonnieres.

Next, we needed to choose the music and the readings for the funeral Mass. Mari suggested the song "Whatsoever you do to the least of my brothers." I thought I already knew why she would make that choice, but I wanted to hear her say it. "Why that song, Mari?"

"Because it describes how we were raised. When I was hungry you gave me to eat. When I was thirsty you gave me to drink. Everyone in the house was fed and given a drink."

I replied, "Yes, I thought so! The song is based on Matthew 25. What do you think about using it as the Gospel reading?"

Mari said, "That's a great idea!"

The songs that we selected were ones that we sang with Frank in San Diego: "Pescador de Hombres," "The Prayer of St. Francis," "Eat This Bread," "Fly Like a Bird," and "On Eagles' Wings." Chris agreed to sing the psalm and play Frank's trumpet for the Mass, which would really make it special.

Fr. Paul, a pastor at St. Jude's when we were younger, agreed to be the celebrant for Frank's funeral Mass and dropped by the house to meet with us. Having gone on several vacations with mom and dad over the years he had lots of fond memories of them.

Fr. Paul asked, "Have you decided on the readings yet?"

Mari answered, "Yes, we would like to have Matthew 25:35-40 for the Gospel reading, but we haven't selected the others yet."

Without hesitation, Fr. Paul, chimed in. "Knowing your father, the reading that tells his story the best is the one from 2 Timothy: 'I, Paul, am already being poured out like a libation, and the time of my departure is at hand. I have competed well; I have finished the race; I have kept the faith' (2 Timothy 4:6-7). It was an ancient religious ritual to pour out wine or a strong drink into the ground as a sacrifice. In many ways your father poured himself out for others, and he certainly kept the faith."

Mari, Ellyn, and I all looked at each other and nodded in agreement.

Fr. Paul then said, "The Old Testament reading I would suggest is the one from 1 Kings that describes how Elijah could eat the food of the angels to keep him on his journey for forty days and nights. 'He got up, ate, and drank then strengthened by that food, he walked forty days and forty nights to the mountain of God, Horeb' (1 Kgs 19:8)."

I couldn't help but think it was a comment not only on Frank's faith but also his uncanny ability to pack away large portions of food.

The next day we went to the funeral home to see how Frank looked in the smaller casket. As we walked in the parlor, we were grateful to see him resting in peace. The last eight months had been hard for him. We agreed that he looked just fine in the smaller casket and felt certain that even Frank would think so too. We didn't need the extra-large casket after all. That certainly solved some problems, and with that decision all the arrangements were finalized. We were grateful for our faith and the familiar Catholic rituals that would soon take us from the vigil to the funeral Mass and on to the final committal, the procession that commemorates the completion of Frank's Christian pilgrimage, begun at his baptism, toward the heavenly kingdom. There was comfort in knowing what to expect and that these liturgies would commend Frank to God and would bring comfort and renewed faith for all of us that mourn his loss.

We arrived early at the funeral home for the wake so the granddaughters could string the carnations. Though it was the smaller casket, it still added a nice touch. As the people started streaming in, I carefully interlaced into Frank's fingers a green rosary with a shamrock imprinted on each of the beads. We were greeted and comforted by many friends and family. Aunt Nancy, Uncle Johnny, and all the cousins came. Lifelong friends, the Schmidts, Foleys, Mannions, and the Whelleys were there to support us. It was a great comfort to see the men's lunch group, their spouses, and friends from St. Jude's Church. There were representatives from every circle of friends that Frank had touched: parishioners, swim buddies, physical therapists, insurance salesmen, college and high school friends. He had made a difference in their lives, and they came to pray for him and his family. As Deacon Kovach, from St. Jude's, led us in the prayers for the Vigil for the Deceased, we turned our hearts and minds to God in praise for the wonderful creation of Frank, to pray for his reception into the heavenly banquet, and for the comfort of all the gathered faithful.

Before we left for the night, we gazed lovingly upon dad and could only smile. He looked so handsome and so at home in his kelly green tie and boutonniere, shamrock rosary beads, and the colors of the Irish flag in carnations draped across the back of the coffin. I was certain that he was smiling right back at us.

Prayer of St. Francis

Lord make me an instrument of Your peace
Where there is hatred let me sow love.
Where there is injury, pardon.
Where there is doubt, faith.
Where there is despair, hope.
Where there is darkness, light.
Where there is sadness joy.
O Divine master grant that I may
Not so much seek to be consoled as to console
To be understood, as to understand.
To be loved. as to love
For it's in giving that we receive
And it's in pardoning that we are pardoned
And it's in dying that we are born. . .
To eternal life.

Chapter 35

The Funeral Mass for John Francis Joseph Madden

And he will raise you up on eagle's wings,
bear you on the breath of dawn,
make you to shine like the sun,
and hold you in the palm of his hand.

Fr. Jan Michael Joncas

O nce more, the Madden family caravan, following the hearse, slowly processed through Mountain Top from the funeral home to St. Jude's Church. It gave us great consolation to return to St. Jude's to celebrate the Funeral Mass for John Francis Joseph Madden with our family, friends, and the Mountain Top community. Gathered together, we could worship God and give thanks for the wondrous creation of Frank Madden.

At the threshold of the church, celebrating the Reception of the Body, Fr. Paul sprinkled Holy Water over Frank's casket. Then his daughters and granddaughters, wearing their green corsages, lovingly draped the white pall over it. His sons-in-law and grandson, wearing their green boutonnieres and ties, and his three nephews guided the casket slowly down the center aisle towards the Eucharistic table.

In the front pew, I stood next to Peter, holding onto his hand as the Gospel was proclaimed. When I heard the words, "For I was hungry and you gave me food, I was thirsty and you gave me drink, a stranger and you welcomed me, naked and you clothed me, ill and you cared for me" (Mt 25:35-36) I squeezed Peter's hand and whispered, "These words are for you! This is what you did!"

Peter did all that and more. In doing the work of a Christian, in fact, Peter was caring for Christ, "Amen, I say to you, whatever you did for one of these least brothers of mine, you did for me" (Mt 25:40).

After Holy Communion, I was invited to share some words of remembrance about Frank. It was such an honor to be able to talk about my father, yet I felt like I had a responsibility to convey what his faith meant to him and how he witnessed it to those around him particularly in his last months. With a sense of gratitude and purpose, I made my way up to the sanctuary and shared the following:

Before I begin, I need to tell you a little story about a man named Francis.

Francis lived in the old country and one night he met his two lads in the pub as he had for many years and made an announcement. "Well, me lads, I am sorry to say that I'll be off to America to be with me daughter in California. But not to worry, whenever we drink, we drink as one."

Off he went to California and soon enough Francis finds his new local pub, O'Sullivan's. As he walks into the pub, Tim, the bartender, says, "Well certainly you are new here. What is your name and what will you have?"

"Francis is me name and I'll be having three pints."

Tim gives him a look and says, "Well now, I can certainly give you your three pints all at once, but we are friendly here, I'd be just as happy to give you one at a time."

Francis says, "Well that's awfully kind of you, but you see when I left the old country, I promised me lads that whenever we'd drink, we'd drink as one. So, if it's all the same to you, I'd like the three pints all at once."

Tim was happy to oblige Francis with his pints as any good bartender would do. So, out come the three pints, down go the three pints, and out goes Francis. Sure enough, this went on night after night, week after week. In goes Francis, out come the three pints, down go the three pints, and out goes Francis. Then early in March Francis walks into the pub, sits down, and says, "Slow down there Tim, I'll only be having two pints tonight!"

A hush went over O'Sullivan's. There was not a dry eye in the place. After Francis finished the two pints, Tim slowly comes up to Francis and says, "Francis, we are all so sorry to hear about the loss of one of your lads."

"Oh, no!" says Francis, "me lads are fine! I've just given up the drink for Lent."

Frank, as you know, was sad to leave you six months ago. I wish I could tell you that he was in the pub "drinking as one" with you, but I can say that he did have you all in his heart. At 6'6" Frank was a big man, big hands, big feet, but it was his heart that was the biggest of all. He had room in it for all of you. He treasured your friendship and support. He loved all the cards, gifts, phone calls, and prayers that came pouring in over the months. It was like living with a celebrity.

The claddagh is a favorite symbol of the Irish, with a great big heart in the center of two hands and a crown on top. The crown stands for loyalty, the heart for love and the hands for friendship. It's a great symbol for us to remember Frank by. He generously offered all of us his love, loyalty, and friendship. Being with Frank in these last months, I am certain that the source of his strength and all that he offered us, came from the love, loyalty, and friendship he had with the Lord. That was the source that always kept him going, the reason Frank never quit. He never gave up on his "Keep at it, Riley!" motto. I want to let you know that he fought hard to the very end, until the moment he asked to go home. He said, "I want to go home." I have no doubt that he wanted to go home to God and to be with Joan. But he certainly wanted to be brought back here with all of you today for this celebration of the Eucharist, the source and summit of our faith, that renews our hope in the resurrection. As Jesus tells us, "I am the living bread that came down from heaven; whoever eats this bread will live forever; and the bread that I will give is my flesh for the life of the world" (Jn 6:51).

And Frank wanted to be one with you again in this Eucharistic celebration. For whenever we celebrate the Eucharist, we celebrate as one. In Eucharistic Prayer II we pray "Humbly we pray that, partaking of the Body and Blood of Christ, we may be gathered into one by the Holy Spirit." So let us remember that in the Eucharist, we are one in Christ with those here on earth and with those that have gone before us in faith. We are still one with Frank and Joan and all our loved ones.

And we can be sure that Frank is already pouring the pints for us up in heaven, awaiting our arrival. And . . . good news . . . there'll be no Lent in heaven!

He Is Gone

You can shed tears that he is gone
Or you can smile because he has lived

You can close your eyes and pray that he will come back
Or you can open your eyes and see all that he has left

Your heart can be empty because you can't see him
Or you can be full of the love that you shared

You can turn your back on tomorrow and live yesterday
Or you can be happy for tomorrow because of yesterday

You can remember him and only that he is gone
Or you can cherish his memory and let it live on

You can cry and close your mind, be empty and turn your back
Or you can do what he would want: smile, open your eyes, love and go on.

David Harkins

ᛗ

Chapter 36

Poured out Like a Libation

I, Paul, am already being poured out like a libation,
and the time of my departure is at hand.
I have competed well; I have finished the race; I have kept the faith.

From now on the crown of righteousness awaits me,
which the Lord, the just judge, will award to me on that day,
and not only to me, but to all who have longed for his appearance.

(2 Tm 4: 6-8, 17-18)

We processed in a caravan from St. Jude's Church to St. Mary's Cemetery. The Rite of Committal was celebrated in the cemetery chapel by Fr. Paul. Afterwards, I invited everyone to join us, as they were able, at the graveside for one last goodbye.

The sons-in-law, grandson, and three nephews carried Frank across the field to the gravesite. I followed behind, linking arms with my two beautiful daughters as the bagpiper accompanied us, playing *Sally Garden*.

Arriving at the graveside we prepared to make a toast to Frank. Chris had a handle of Jameson's, and green plastic shot glasses for everyone. It seemed to take an eternity to pour out shots for all thirty people gathered around the grave. I am not sure this was my finest moment, but all of a sudden, I could hear myself saying in a fake Irish brogue:

Mike says to Pat one night in the pub:

"Well, Pat, I have a thought here. The good Lord knows we've been drinkin' together night after night, year after year. So, don't you think it's only fitting then that when one of us goes, the other pours a pint out on the other lad's grave?"

"Ah Mike, tis' a grand idea."

Wouldn't you know it, only a month goes by, and Mike leaves this world to go up to the pearly gates.

Sure enough, there is Pat, loyal friend and drinking companion, standing at Mike's gravesite, raising a pint.

"Mike, here you go lad, here is your pint, just as I promised. But, Mike, would you mind if I run it through me kidneys first?"

There was a mix of reactions—some gasped, a few laughed. I am certain Frank loved it. Fortunately, just in time, the shots were all poured. I raised my glass and said, "To Frank!"

Everyone joined me in raising their glasses as I sang the Irish Blessing. As we drank our shots of Jameson, Mari poured hers over the casket saying, "Well, here you go, Frank!"

In his beautiful voice, Peter blessed us with a most heart-tugging rendition of "Danny Boy." As if that wasn't already perfect, the bagpiper played the Notre Dame fight song as we all filed passed the casket for our last goodbyes and took our leave to go to the luncheon.

As I waited to be the last to leave, out of the corner of my eye I saw a gentleman in work pants and a t-shirt with the fighting Irish leprechaun on it. When I noticed the tears in his eyes, I offered him a shot. He replied, "I'm sorry

ma'am. I can't. I'm working. I'm a grave digger. But did you
know, I was here for your mother's burial too?"
    "Oh, Thank you. God bless you for all you do."
    "He does."

Danny Boy

Oh, Danny boy, the pipes, the pipes are calling
From glen to glen, and down the mountain side.
The summer's gone, and all the roses falling,
It's you, it's you must go and I must bide.
But come ye back when summer's in the meadow,
Or when the valley's hushed and white with snow,
It's I'll be there in sunshine or in shadow,—
Oh, Danny boy, Oh Danny boy, I love you so!

But when ye come, and all the flowers are dying,
If I am dead, as dead I well may be,
Ye'll come and find the place where I am lying,
And kneel and say an Avé there for me.
And I shall hear, though soft you tread above me,
And all my grave will warmer, sweeter be,
For you will bend
and tell me that you love me,
And I shall sleep in peace until you come to me!

Frederick E. Weatherly

Chapter 37

The Irish Goodbye

Following our ritual pattern for funeral celebrations, everyone was invited to the luncheon at Genetti's after the burial. Just to simplify our planning, we had the same food and same setup that we had for mom's. What was different was the microphone. Ordinarily for my family, it is safest to hide all microphones. Everyone has something to say (at least once) and takes a long time to do it. For Frank, however, we decided to break tradition and invite people to share their thoughts and stories. There were some gems, some funny, some sad. Then the sons-in-law started to take turns and eventually the microphone was handed to Peter. Unwilling at first but feeling a bit of pressure to say something, he began to share his heartfelt story about Frank.

> I am the only one of Frank's sons-in-law without Irish heritage. It was always a huge disappointment for Frank, which is why perhaps from very early on he converted my good Scottish name to Irish by pronouncing it McGuinness, like the beer. I got him back though by giving his daughter a nice McInnes tartan clan scarf for her to wear. That did not go over well. Suffice it to say, we both got "the look." Nevertheless,

Frank and I made it work. The kegerator in the garage certainly helped.

Peter paused for a long moment.

You know, many think that it was a hardship for us to care for Frank. I have to admit that I had my concerns about the plan. Frank was an invalid. He had an amazing number of health issues. He was traveling far from his beloved Mountain Top. It was going to be a huge disruption to our lives.

Another pause. Peter continued, his voice wavering with emotion.

Welcoming Frank into our home turned out to be one of the best things that ever happened to me. My children got the opportunity to spend time with their grandfather that they never had due to the distance. Noreen and Frank broadened and deepened their relationship. I had the chance to better know a man whose strength and good humor amazed me on a daily basis. It was one of the biggest blessings of my life.

Peter raised his glass: "To Frank."

There wasn't a dry eye in the room. We had seen what an amazing impact Frank had on Peter. I knew how amazing Peter was to Frank.

The lunch migrated from Genetti's to the house in Mountain Top. The story swapping and the libations continued well into the night. The beer pong tournaments on the back porch were multi-generational, each age group having their own set of skills to boast about.

The "Irish Goodbye" was the accepted ritual for ending the evening. It's an Irish American custom of just ducking out from a party without saying a proper good-bye. We excuse it as a holdover from the Great Famine days when some of our ancestors just jumped on a boat to escape the long-drawn-out emotional good-bye, never to be heard from again. Today there was too much to be said, too much to cry about. Just slipping out may have been the better way.

The Parting Glass

Of all the money that e'er I had
I spent it in good company
And all the harm I've ever done
Alas, it was to none but me

And all I've done for want of wit
To memory now I can't recall
So fill to me the parting glass
Good night and joy be to you all

So fill to me the parting glass
And drink a health whate'er befalls
Then gently rise and softly call
Good night and joy be to you all

Chapter 38

The Thin Place

After the celebration of the funeral liturgies in Mountain Top it was difficult to return to an empty house in San Diego. We missed Frank so much. The silence was disturbing after having so much activity in our house for the past six months. All of Frank's support team, streaming in and out, were now gone. These beloved people were not able to take part in any of the Mountain Top celebrations. We felt the need to welcome them back into this space once more, to thank God for them, for their amazing ministry, and to thank God for Frank. Fr. Joe, our associate pastor, agreed to celebrate a memorial Mass for Frank in our home. It was the perfect way to lift our prayers and hearts to God and to give thanks, especially since Eucharist means thanksgiving.

There is a lovely Irish tradition called the month's mind, where close family and friends celebrate a memorial Mass for their deceased loved one followed by a meal one month after their death. It is a more intimate celebration that is distanced from the initial shock and pain from the loss. In a way our San Diego celebration was a variation of the month's mind.

Frank's doctors, nurses, aides, neighbors, and friends gathered in our living room where Frank had received the

Eucharist many times. We read the same scriptures and sang the same songs as we had at Frank's funeral. After Mass, in Frank's room—the dining room—we spread a lavish buffet of grilled tri-tip, Mrs. Suttman's potatoes, fruit salad, and a green salad.

"Pretty Mary" was there. That was Frank's nickname for the special nurse practitioner who worked with Frank's pulmonologist. She shared with me that she had counseled Frank in the hospital about his serious medical condition and what his options were.

"Noreen, I told Frank, due to the condition of his lungs, if he struggled to breathe, he would be intubated and placed on a ventilator. Since his lungs were very weak, it was not likely that he would improve or recover enough to ever be taken off the machine. That meant that at the end of his life he wouldn't be able to speak or eat by mouth, two things he was quite fond of. I was honest with him. I told him that he didn't have long. Then Frank just quietly said to me, 'OK, but we don't have to tell Noreen that do we?'"

"Oh, Mary," I drew in a deep breath. "Thank you for sharing that with me. Thank you for being honest with Frank. I think he needed to hear that, though it must have been hard for him to bear such heavy news on his own." Tears welled up in my eyes. "He was still trying to take care of me. But I understand his time had come and he understood that as well."

"Noreen, his body was letting us know that it was winding down and he was getting ready to be with his Lord and Savior. Unfortunately, the medical community does not always recognize that someone is preparing to pass and instead of seeing this as a normal part of our human journey, attempts to extend life with futile medicine, causing undue suffering that prolongs the dying process. Oh . . . lovely Frank . . . always made me blush when he called me 'Pretty

Mary.' I am so happy you were able to bring him home with hospice to be comfortable and to find his way to the Lord."

Tears streaming down my face, I looked into her eyes and whispered, "Mary, thank you for taking such good care of Frank and having an honest conversation with him exactly at the moment he was ready for it. We are tremendously blessed that Frank was able to make all the decisions about his care and that he was able to let go, let God, on his own. It meant so much to us to have him home when he passed, so peacefully. It was such a gift."

At the end of the meal, as a thank you gift, everyone received a glass. It was etched with the claddagh on one side and on the other, Frank's name, the date of his birth on earth, and the date of his birth into heaven, which we continue to celebrate on each anniversary. And of course, the glass reminds us all to "Keep at it, Riley!"

Frank J. Madden,
02/04/30 ~06/24/13
Keep at it, Riley!

After filling each glass with the guest's choice of a shot of Jameson's or water we raised them up for a toast and an Irish Blessing to Frank.

In the mystical realm of Celtic spirituality, there are *Thin Places* where one can catch a glimpse of the divine, where only a thin veil separates heaven and earth. It is a place where one can easily pass from one side to the other. It seemed fitting then, that here in this thin place we would celebrate a memorial Mass, a thanksgiving, where bread and wine become the Body and Blood of Christ, where the angels had come for Frank, where heaven and earth had touched.

The Veil Was Torn

Jesus cried out again in a loud voice, and gave up his spirit.
And behold, the veil of the sanctuary was torn in two
from top to bottom.
The earth quaked, rocks were split, tombs were opened,
and the bodies of many saints who had fallen asleep were raised.
And coming forth from their tombs after his resurrection,
they entered the holy city and appeared to many.
The centurion and the men with him
who were keeping watch over Jesus
feared greatly when they saw the earthquake
and all that was happening, and they said,
"Truly, this was the Son of God!"

(Mt 27:50-54)

Chapter 39

The Blessings

W hen does life begin? That proves to be a difficult question for many. So, Trinity College Dublin invited a minister, a priest, and a rabbi for an inter-faith theological debate on the topic.

The moderator began, "Thank you everyone for coming this afternoon as we attempt to tackle the difficult question, 'When does life begin?' Minister Smith, we'd like to start with you, when do you say that life begins?"

Minister Smith replied, "Well, that is very challenging to pinpoint, because it's more of a quickening."

"Ah, I see. Well, Fr. O'Malley, what do you have to say? When does life begin?"

Fr. O'Malley responded, "It's very simple, life begins at conception. That's all there is to it."

"Rabbi Schwartz, when do you say that life begins?"

Rabbi Schwartz replied confidently, "Oh yes, that is an easy one. Life begins when all the kids have left the house, and the dog dies."

There is some obvious truth to that joke, which signaled that—considering the age of our children and our dogs—before Frank came to live with us life seemed about to begin for Peter and me. But in the upside-down wisdom of God, it wasn't emptying our home that brought us "life." Filling it did. In many ways, welcoming Frank into our home was when life began for us. It was truly a gift and a blessing to accompany Frank during his last days. He encouraged us all to be the best version of ourselves even if it meant to keep studying after others had turned in for the night. Everyone Frank met was encouraged to "Keep at it, Riley!" and were blessed abundantly with the wisdom of that motto.

THE THREE DAUGHTERS

The three Madden daughters inherited very different sets of talents and received the education to develop them for law, medicine, and liturgy. It took the marriage of our skills and talents to work collaboratively in caring for Frank and settling his affairs. All those years when our parents lived in Pennsylvania, Mari shouldered most of the responsibilities. After Frank left the East Coast, Mari continued to maintain their house and concerns while Ellyn and I took on the California care. May Joan and Frank's blood continue to course through our veins and through our descendants to serve the people of God as Joan and Frank did so well, for so many, and for so long. Slainte!

REYNALDO

Frank always called Reynaldo "Mando," or "Mighty Mouse." "Big Frank" was almost three times the size of Reynaldo. But Reynaldo never complained. He worked very hard, spending many days and nights in our home taking care of Frank and us too. Every night he was at our home, Reynaldo joined in saying bedtime prayers and singing hymns. After Frank died, Reynaldo went on to take care of several dying priests. I'm sure that Reynaldo, a very holy man, was a tremendous blessing to them.

BRIAN

When Brian arrived at our door, he had just moved from New York City to California, intending to "figure things out." He was an excellent Certified Nursing Assistant, but we could easily see that Brian had been given many untapped gifts. We were just a stopping point in his life. He is now in medical school, on his way to becoming a psychiatrist. He was a blessing to us and will certainly be one to all his future patients.

SERGIO

Frank did not like it that Sergio lived with his girlfriend. He'd say, "Make an honest woman out of her! You need to marry that girl."

After Frank died, Sergio did just that. He married his girlfriend, and the next year, on Frank's birthday, they were blessed with beautiful twin girls! And now they also have a handsome son. Sergio is currently working on finishing his RN degree and plans to go on to become a Physician's Assistant. Sergio was very smart, organized, and wonderful to be around. We are so happy that he will be in a position to use the many gifts he has been given.

THE BILLS

Frank was an insurance salesman and had always assured us that he had excellent health coverage. Frank, however, didn't know much more than that, since it was mom who kept track of the money. After she died, we scoured the house and found two policies. When I called the insurance companies up to ask what they covered, I was told to submit the claims to find out. I didn't see how that could be legal, but that's what we started doing. It took three of us to handle all the paperwork and bills. I focused on Frank's care, Peter paid the bills, and Ellyn was the point of contact with the insurance companies and submitted the claims. This was way more difficult than it appears. Fortunately, Peter had a very organized system to track claims as they were submitted and when they had been processed. Peter would ask Ellyn to follow up on the claims that were denied or seemingly ignored by the insurance company. As a nurse, she knew the right lingo and what buttons to push. Some claims had to be resubmitted two or three times before they were paid. Eventually we figured out that the CNAs were covered with one policy and the LVNs with the other.

After Frank died, the insurance companies immediately stopped processing all claims. Ellyn had to badger them with many phone calls and letters of complaint before they began to respond. I couldn't help wondering how many claims fall through the cracks after an elderly patient dies and are never reimbursed unless there's an advocate like Ellyn to challenge the insurance companies. In the end, with a lot of persistence and a "Keep at it, Riley!" attitude, every bill was reimbursed! We were only responsible for a modest deductible to have all that health care in our home.

THE HEALING CHAIR

Frank's lift chair was disassembled in Mountain Top by Jack Costigan, loaded onto the medical coach, driven across the country, and reassembled in our family room. Unfortunately, because he mostly needed the wheelchair, Frank sat in it fewer than a dozen times. Though it might appear that moving the chair to San Diego was useless, it has proved otherwise. We now call it the "healing chair."

It has come to the rescue for many of us as we recovered from various illnesses and surgeries. Anyone that has to sleep sitting up after a procedure, elevate their legs, or needs assistance getting in and out of a chair uses it. When the call comes that the chair is needed, Shaun, Dave, and Peter move into action. They load it onto Shaun's truck and deliver it to the next patient.

Hollianne always keeps her eye out for anyone in the parish in need of the healing chair. Mary used it after lung surgery; her daughter, Claire slept in it for two weeks after surgery to correct a *pectus excavatum* (sunken breast-bone). Mollie elevated her leg after her dislocated patella was repaired, and I needed it to recover after I fractured my patella. We all healed well—and in style—thanks to the "healing chair," and thanks to Frank and Jack.

THE THESIS

When my mother's former student handed me his doctoral thesis on the steps of St. Jude's, I didn't know who it was meant for. Who is best at math? I still can't answer that, but my mother had certainly left a legacy that highly valued education. From the time she was thirteen, she had a burning desire to go to college, but her father, a fire-fighter, was out on disability after successive heart attacks. She could afford college only if she won the scholarship for being first in her high school graduating class, and that she did. She told me her father would throw more coal on the fire in the kitchen stove to keep it warm for her as she stayed up late into the night, studying. She had her own version of "Keep at it, Riley!"

Since Frank's death, his family has been blessed with educational opportunities and great success. As he would often say, "There's a lot of Madden in those kids!" Those nights that my grandfather told Frank to "Keep at it, Riley!" have certainly borne fruit in his offspring. At the risk of sounding like an annoying braggadocious Christmas letter, I will share the list of degrees earned by Frank and Joan's grandchildren:

Mari's daughter—

Aileen: BA, Psychology and Spanish, Temple University; Psy.D., Clinical Psychology, Loyola University, Maryland

Ellyn's daughters—

Riley: BS, Biology, UC Santa Barbara; DPT, Northwestern University

Haley: BS Design, Graphic Design, Arizona State University

My children—

Mollie: BS, Mechanical Engineering, Northeastern University

Kelley: BBA Finance and Information Systems Quantitative Management, Loyola Marymount University; Micro-Masters, Supply Chain, Massachusetts Institute of Technology

Greg: PhD, Biomedical Informatics, Stanford University

PETER

Peter was the rock, the one behind the scenes that made it possible to care for Frank in our home. He installed ramps, an outdoor shower, curtains, and a TV in the dining room. He did the grocery shopping and eventually all the cooking for the clan of people in the house.

Truly, Peter was the Gospel of Matthew 25 incarnate. He fed, clothed, sheltered, and took care of Frank when he was ill. He was most generous with his time, his home, and his wife. Peter was always there to support me and encourage me to keep going when I doubted myself. None of what came about would have happened without him.

Frank prayed every night while he was in our home that Peter would turn Catholic, and I know he had been praying since we were engaged thirty years earlier. Two years after Frank's death, seemingly out of the blue, Peter said to me, "I'd like to be baptized." You can imagine how that rocked my world! I had been praying for thirty years too. On the Vigil of Pentecost, in 2016, I sobbed with joy as Peter received the sacraments of Christian initiation. I am thankful every day for this tremendous blessing for him and for me.

If It Dies, It Produces Much Fruit

Amen, amen, I say to you,
unless a grain of wheat falls to the ground and dies,
it remains just a grain of wheat;
but if it dies, it produces much fruit.

Whoever loves his life loses it,
and whoever hates his life in this world
will preserve it for eternal life.

Whoever serves me must follow me,
and where I am, there also will my servant be.
The Father will honor whoever serves me.

(Jn 12:24-26)

Chapter 40

Love Is the Answer

St. Patrick's Day, 2013.
Murphy, Sophie, Noreen, Frank, and Kona

Frank was certain that I would need a puppy to help me deal with the death of my "fur child" Kona. Her time had obviously been drawing near. Would her loss be difficult for me? Well, let's just say, when I had teenagers in the house, I treasured the fact that Kona *never* rolled her eyes at me. Not even once! She never complained about what was for dinner. If dinner was late, she was even happier to get it when it finally arrived. What's not to love?

Maybe it was insanity, or maybe it was great wisdom when Murphy became a part of our family. From the moment Murphy arrived he turned on his charm. He seemed to know when we needed a smile, and his antics never let us down. Frank and Murphy were fast friends. Murphy liked to lie in the flower bed next to the window right alongside Frank's bed. It was a great spot since they could keep an eye on each other from there. Frank took Murphy with him on his "walks" around the neighborhood. It was great entertainment because Murphy never walked; he only pranced. Neighbors would often stop and comment, "What a good-lookin' dog he is." And of course, at mealtimes the two of them were inseparable since Murphy was guaranteed a sample from Frank's plate.

When I came back to our empty house after Frank's funeral in Pennsylvania, it was Murphy who greeted me and made me smile. Murphy was there to distract me, not from Kona's death, but Frank's. My sweet Kona lived on happily for another three months.

Soon after, Murphy had grown into a one hundred pound large-and-in-charge dog who seemed determined to protect me from the world. Did Frank have this in mind? At that size and with his protective temperament, Murphy became a challenge to walk. Unfortunately, when Murphy was a puppy, it was necessary to put aside his training to focus on Frank.

Early one morning I snuck out of the house to walk Murphy before any other dogs were out in the neighborhood. Walking Murphy, I had to be hypervigilant, always on edge, and ready to cross the street to avoid another dog. Murphy had a way of snarling that made it really clear to other dogs that they needed to back off. He was all bark and no bite, but I didn't want to take any chances; so I kept him on a tight leash.

As I walked, I decided that it was time to get Murphy sorted out. But what to do? Do I take him to a training class that guarantees a good outcome but uses a shock collar? Or do I keep up the positive reinforcement?

Remembering all the walks I took with Frank, I wished so badly that I could do that again today. Frank was always happy to talk problems through, especially when it was about dogs or cars. Hmm, could I still walk with him now? Could he be with me even though he's gone?

I started praying the rosary as I walked. It was a Wednesday, the day to say the Glorious Mysteries, so I started the decade for the Resurrection. As I reached the park, I could see down along the way an older man with a shock of white hair and a French bulldog were approaching. I quickly moved off the path to give them a wide berth. But as we neared each other, the man shouted predictably, "That's some good-lookin' dog." So, we started to chat, and I got to know Andrew and Charlie, and had a wonderful conversation. Surprisingly, Murphy sat calmly without any snarling. When Andrew noticed the gentle leader wrapped around Murphy's muzzle he asked, "What's with the leash? Are you having trouble with Mr. Handsome, there?"

"Well, yes, I am. Thank you for asking! I am really concerned about it. He can get a bit aggressive when we approach another dog and I'm not sure what to do. Some have suggested a shock collar. What do you think?"

"I don't know much in this world, but love is the answer. Love is always the answer."

Somehow, I felt certain that Frank had heard my prayers. I looked up into the heavens and whispered, to Frank, "Keep at it, Riley!"

Love Is the Answer!

Love is patient, love is kind.
It is not jealous, [love] is not pompous, it is not inflated,
it is not rude, it does not seek its own interests,
it is not quick-tempered, it does not brood over injury,
it does not rejoice over wrongdoing but rejoices with the truth.
It bears all things, believes all things,
hopes all things, endures all things.
Love never fails.

(1 Cor 13:4-8)

Epilogue

The Celtic Cross

Where in Ireland did we Maddens come from? After Frank was laid to rest, I was left with a burning desire to answer that question. Was it because Frank had now joined all our family that have gone before us, or was it because I hoped to be with them one day too? For whatever reason, I couldn't rest until I found out more about our Irish heritage.

Whenever I asked Frank where the Maddens came from, he'd say County Mayo. But did that come from a surname map of Irish roots? Or was that information handed down from his father?

After a bit of digging through handwritten census records, I was surprised to find out that my second great grandfather, John Madden, was from Killybrackey, County Tyrone. But County Tyrone is in Northern Ireland. What? Uh-oh! Did that mean we are Protestant?

Peter and I set off for Ireland to see what we could discover. Wandering up and down the green hills and dales of Northern Ireland we came across a sign that said "Killybrackey." Since there were only a few houses in the small town, I bravely knocked on a door. As it opened, I was met by an older gentleman dressed in a cream-colored Irish knit sweater and grey slacks. He greeted me with his warm smile and steel blue eyes.

"Hi, I'm Noreen Madden. I'm from America. It seems that my Madden family lived here at one time. I'm trying to find any information I can about them."

"I'm Frank Cavanaugh. Would you like to come inside?"

"Well, yes, I would. Thank you." As I followed Frank into his parlor, I spotted a portrait of Pope John Paul II hanging proudly on the wall and sighed with relief.

As we sat in front of his fire, Frank shared that he was eighty years old and on his own now. When he spoke of his relatives in America we felt an unspoken connection, with families and hearts that reached across the pond.

Frank confessed, "I never knew the Maddens, but my father always pointed out the Maddens' land. It's just down the lane here. I could show it to you if you like."

"Oh, yes please, I would like that very much."

As we headed out, Frank dipped his fingers into the holy water font next to the front door and blessed himself. Just a few steps down the gravel path, Frank pointed out a small gate and an overgrown field and said, "Well, there it is." He glanced at me and said, "I hope you are not disappointed."

"Oh Frank, I'm so happy to have found you and this land. This is wonderful. It's much more that I had ever hoped for." Then I pressed further, "Where is the nearest Catholic Church?"

"That would be St. Malachy's, just down the road."

"Do you think they would have any records of the Maddens there?"

Frank answered, "No, you would have to go up to St. Patrick's in Dungannon for that."

As we strolled back down the lane to Frank's house, I found it difficult to put into words the deep connection to Ireland and my ancestors I had received through our brief conversation. "Well Frank, it was so wonderful to meet you. Thank you so much for your kindness. Be well."

Off we went to St. Patrick's Roman Catholic church, and I wandered into the parish office. The lovely and patient parish secretary flipped through some files and within minutes I was staring down at the record proving that my second great grandfather, John Madden, of Killybrackey, was baptized Catholic on May 14, 1822. Then she was able to go one step further and found the record that my third great grandfather, Edward Madden, was baptized Catholic on April 10, 1786.

In 1609 an edict, coinciding with the penal laws, was issued in Dungannon forbidding all practice of the Catholic religion. For nearly two hundred years these draconian laws drove the Church underground. There was no church in the town. Between 1778 and 1793 a number of Roman Catholic Relief Acts were passed in the Irish Parliament, gradually easing the sanctions against Catholics.

The Maddens who came before Edward remained Catholic even though the law forbade it. When Edward and John suffered through the Great Famine, they left these beautiful green hills around 1850 for an unknown land, taking a chance on survival. They certainly lived the "Keep at it, Riley!" motto. I owe them my faith, my strength of will, and my life. But where did the name Riley come from? I honestly don't know. I never found a Riley in any of our family census records. It remains a mystery to this day.

Those that remained in Ireland after the Great Famine still struggled through home evictions, poor health, and hunger as they mourned the loss of those that died and those that emigrated. Yet, it is in dark times such as these that the Blessed Mother has appeared throughout history to comfort the lowly and the suffering in various cultures. And without fail, during a heavy downpour of rain, on the night of August 21, 1879, in Knock, County Mayo, Our Lady appeared to a small handful of people of modest means. She never spoke a single word, yet her miraculous appearance comforted the desperate people of Ireland. Her apparition and that of a lamb and a cross enthroned upon an altar encouraged the Irish to take part more reverently in the Mass and to have a greater love of Jesus in the Blessed Sacrament. The Blessed Mother consistently points us to her son asking us to "Do whatever he tells you" (Jn 2:5).

The Celtic cross, a long cherished Irish symbol of Christian faith and Irish culture, also points us to Christ. The cross with a circle at the intersection of the two beams is said to have originated with St. Patrick when he converted pagans to Christianity. The circle, thought to represent the sun which the pagans worshipped, was integrated with the Christian cross. Perhaps it shows that the Christian God created the sun, and that the true light we follow is the light of Christ. The circle, with no beginning or end, symbolizes the infinite love of God as witnessed by the outpouring of Christ upon the cross for our salvation. At baptism we begin our lives as Christians, dying to ourselves and rising to new life in Christ. Receiving the sacraments throughout our lives, we continue to conform ourselves to the heart of Christ so that we too can be an outpouring of love, sacrificing ourselves for the good of the other.

When Frank asked me the simple question, "Can we be your Africa?" he offered me a profound, life-changing opportunity and a tremendous blessing. I was able to say "yes" in faith because of my baptism. My compass and my strength were the sacraments, the encounter with the living God, the Real Presence of Christ. The Eucharist, the source and summit of our Christian life, is the way, the truth, and the life. Through the Eucharist we can "Keep at it, Riley!"

39

Our Lady of Knock

Our Lady of Knock, Queen of Ireland,
you gave hope to your people in a time of distress
and comforted them in sorrow.
You have inspired countless pilgrims to pray with confidence
to your divine Son, remembering His promise,
"Ask and you shall receive, seek and you shall find."
Help me to remember that we are all pilgrims on the road to Heaven.
Fill me with love and concern for my brothers and sisters in Christ,
especially those who live with me.
Comfort me when I am sick, lonely or depressed.
Teach me how to take part ever more reverently in the Holy Mass.
Give me a greater love of Jesus in the Blessed Sacrament.
Pray for me now and at the end of my death.
Amen.

Afterword

The Irish Blessing

He Emptied Himself

Have among yourselves the same attitude
that is also yours in Christ Jesus,
Who, though he was in the form of God,
did not regard equality with God
something to be grasped.
Rather, he emptied himself, taking the form of a slave,
coming in human likeness;
and found human in appearance, he humbled himself,
becoming obedient to death, even death on a cross.

Phil 2:5-8

The Irish blessing is a favored prayer said when loved ones part, asking that nature be kind and that God will hold us in the hollow of his hands. But to be in God's hands is at once a place of safety and one of sacrifice. Though God is always waiting and wanting to hold us tenderly, we must willingly and vulnerably place ourselves into his hands; to see God as the potter and we, the clay. "LORD, you are our father; we are the clay and you our potter: we are all the work of your hand" (Is 64:7).

At every Mass, through the re-presentation of the Paschal Mystery, Jesus models humble kenosis (self-emptying). Jesus surrendered to the will of his Father in coming to earth as a helpless infant to offer his life on a cross for our salvation. We are also asked to surrender to do the will of the Father, not ours. "For whoever wishes to save his life will lose it, but whoever loses his life for my sake and that of the gospel will save it" (Mk 8:35).

At the Last Supper Jesus said, "This is my body, which will be given for you; do this in memory of me" (Lk 22:19). In response to those words, at every Mass, bread is taken, blessed, broken, and given. We are offered Holy Communion with the words, "The Body of Christ." We respond by saying "Amen," and receive Christ into the hollow of our hands. In this *Thin Place* our "Amen" proclaims that the Blessed Sacrament is the Real Presence of Christ, that *we* are the body of Christ, and that we commit ourselves to serving the body of Christ as Jesus did, on his knees, with a towel and a basin. "If I, therefore, the master and teacher, have washed your feet, you ought to wash one another's feet. I have given you a model to follow, so that as I have done for you, you should also do" (Jn 13:14-15).

We are sent forth from the Mass to bring Christ to the world. We are called to be Christ for others each day of our lives, in sickness and in health, until the angels come to take us home.

Croagh Patrick, the Holy Mountain of Ireland, rises 2,500 ft
above Clew Bay in County Mayo.

According to tradition, in 441 AD, St. Patrick prayed and fasted for
forty days, surrendering his will, on this mountain top, in preparation for his ministry to convert Ireland to Christianity.

Locally known as "the Reek," this mountain remains
a popular pilgrimage site with thousands climbing it
on the last Sunday of July or "Reek Sunday."

Peter and I climbed Croagh Patrick the summer
after Frank was laid to rest.

Frank J. Madden
02/04/30 ~06/24/13
Keep at it, Riley!

Notes

1. Scripture texts in this work are taken from the New American Bible, revised edition © 2010, 1991, 1986, 1970 Confraternity of Christian Doctrine, Washington, D.C. and are used by permission of the copyright owner. All Rights Reserved.

2. *Pastoral Care of the Sick: Rites of Anointing and Viaticum*, in *The Rites of the Catholic Church as Revised by the Second Vatican Ecumenical Council*, vol. 1 (Collegeville: The Liturgical Press, 1990), 759-908. Hereafter *PCS*.

3. St. Patrick, "The Confession," in *St. Patrick: The Real Story*, ed. and trans. Jim Mc Cormack CM (Blackrock: The Columba Press, 2008), 11.

4. *The Roman Missal Renewed by Decree of the Most Holy Second Ecumenical Council of the Vatican, Promulgated by Authority of Pope Paul VI and Revised at the Direction of Pope John Paul II. For Use in the Dioceses of the United States of America.* Third Typical Edition (New Jersey: Catholic Book Publishing Corp., 2011) no. 115. Hereafter, *Roman Missal*.

5   Roberto Ferruzzi, Madonna of the Streets. Aquinat, created this photo from the 2-dimensional picture Madonnina (painting), Public Domain, https://commons.wikimedia.org/w/index.php?curid=15857775

6. *Order of Christian Funerals with Cremation Rite, Revised by Decree of the Second Vatican Council and Published by Authority of Pope Paul VI*, (New Jersey: Catholic Book Publishing Corp., 2019), no. 206. Hereafter OCF.

7. OCF, nos. 174 -176.

8. The Golden Dome atop the Main Building at the University of Notre Dame. (Photo: Rebecca DeLev / Shutterstock)

9. Charles C. Camosy, *Losing Our Dignity: How Secularized Medicine is Undermining Fundamental Human Equality* (Hyde Park: New City Press, 2021), 83-86.

10. "Understanding Do Not Resuscitate Orders (DNR)", Advanced Care Directives, Mass General Brigham, Brigham and Women's Faulkner Hospital, 2021, https://www.brighamandwomensfaulkner.org/patients-and-families/advance-care-directives/dnr-orders.

11. *Roman Missal*, Easter Preface.

12. *Catechism of the Catholic Church*, nos. 1011-1012. Hereafter CCC.

13. Claire Santry, "Coffin ships: death and pestilence on the Atlantic," Irish Genealogy Toolkit, https://www.irish-genealogy-toolkit.com/coffin-ships.html.

14. PCS, no. 199.

15. PCS, no. 175.

16. St. Brendan, *The Voyage of St. Brendan: The Navigator*, trans. Gerard McNamara (self-pub., CreateSpace, 2013), 12.

17. St. Brendan, 19.

18. Coalition for Compassionate Care of California, Physician Orders for Life Sustaining Treatment, POLST California, 2021, https://capolst.org/.

19. Martin Tobin, MD, Constantine Manthous, MD. Reviewers: Catherine Chen, MD, Ann C. Jennerich, MD, MS, Hrishkesh S. Kulkarni, MD, Marianna Sockrider, MD, DrPH, Kevin Wilson, MD, "Mechanical Ventilation," Patient Information: Education Series, American Thoracic Society, April 2020, https://www.thoracic.org/patients/patient-resources/resources/mechanical-ventilation.pdf.

20. Camosy, 86.

21. PCS, nos. 42-296. PCS includes rites for Visiting the Sick, Communion of the Sick, Anointing of the Sick, Viaticum, Commendation of the Dying, Prayers for the Dead, and Rites for Exceptional Circumstances.

22. Second Vatican Council, Constitution *Sacrosanctum Concilium* (*The Sacred Liturgy*), Dec. 4, 1963, no. 7, http://www.vatican.va/archive/hist_councils/ii_vatican_council/documents/vat-ii_const_19631204_sacrosanctum-concilium_en.html. Hereafter Sacrosanctum Concilium.

23. PCS, nos. 81-91. The Communion of the Sick: Communion in Ordinary Circumstances is well suited for the sick and homebound in a residential living situation.

24. PCS, nos. 92-96. The Communion of the Sick: Communion in a Hospital or Institution is best suited to situations where an abbreviated rite is needed to minster to multiple communicants with serious illness.

25 *Sacrosanctum Concilium*, no. 8. "In the earthly liturgy we take part in a foretaste of that heavenly liturgy which is celebrated in the holy city of Jerusalem toward which we journey as pilgrims, where Christ is sitting at the right hand of God, a minister of the holies and of the true tabernacle."

26. Pope Francis, Apostolic Exhortation *Evangelii Gaudium (On the Proclamation of the Gospel in Today's World)*, Nov. 24, 2013, no. 266, Holy See, https://www.vatican.va/content/francesco/en/apost_exhortations/documents/papa-francesco_esortazione-ap_20131124_evangelii-gaudium.html.

27. St. Leo the Great Sermon 74, 2:PL 54, 398. Cited in CCC, no. 1115.

28. PCS, no. 175.

29. *Sacrosanctum Concilium*, no. 73.

30. PCS, nos. 10-11.

31. PCS, nos. 223-231. The Prayers for the Dead, Anointing is only for the living, yet the dead are helped by the prayers of the living.

32. PCS, no. 98.

33. CCC, no. 1532.

34. PCS, no. 124.

35. PCS, no. 102.

36. At the Diocesan Chrism Mass, the bishop blesses the Oil of the Sick by saying this prayer. The oil is used for the Sacrament the Anointing of the Sick throughout the diocese during that year (The Order of Blessing the Oil of Catechumens and of the Sick and of Consecrating the Chrism, 20).

37. Commendation of the Dying, Litany B. and Prayer of Commendation B., PCS, nos. 219-220.

38. PCS, nos. 175-211. There are two rites for the celebration of Viaticum, the last sacrament of Christian life, Viaticum within Mass and Viaticum outside Mass.

39. Barbara Walsh, "Sunset," https://www.flickr.com/photos/barbarawalsh/5558938174/in/photostream/.

New City Press

New City Press is one of more than 20 publishing houses sponsored by the Focolare, a movement founded by Chiara Lubich to help bring about the realization of Jesus' prayer: "That all may be one" (John 17:21). In view of that goal, New City Press publishes books and resources that enrich the lives of people and help all to strive toward the unity of the entire human family. We are a member of the Association of Catholic Publishers.

www.newcitypress.com
202 Comforter Blvd.
Hyde Park, New York

Periodicals
Living City Magazine
www.livingcitymagazine.com

Scan to join our mailing list for discounts and promotions or go to www.newcitypress.com and click on "join our email list."